Further Praise for *The Place You Love Is Gone*

"As deeply felt as it is intellectually wide-ranging, this book allows us to listen in on a fascinating, cultivated, poetic consciousness as it chews on the big and small issues of place and self. A delightful exploration by a singularly alert author." —Phillip Lopate

"A compelling blend of memoir and survey of growth planning and change." —*Midwest Book Review*

"I was born and raised in Akron, Ohio, just like Melissa Holbrook Pierson. She deftly sidesteps nostalgia to mix sadness with historical insight in her new book. It struck resonant chords in me, reverberating somewhere between memory and loss."

—Jim Jarmusch

"Melissa Pierson uses her lyrical gifts to make us look at the American penchant for moving on from a place once loved and see the price of our too-easy resolutions of loss. As usual, her writing is both lovely and incisive."

—Christine Stansell, professor of history, Princeton University, and author of *American Moderns*

"A keen eye and wry sense of humor." —*Kirkus Reviews*

"A graceful and deeply wise elegy for a nation that cannot stop systematically destroying any place that was ever worth caring about. Her prose is moving, beautifully constructed, and sure to connect with countless hearts broken over the loss of the places they loved." —James Howard Kunstler, author of *The Long Emergency*

"Melissa Holbrook Pierson mourns the loss of diverse American landscapes. She writes with passion. . . . Anyone who cares about the sense of place and human scale of buildings will identify with her definition of home in this wonderful, personal book."

—Dolores Hayden, author of *A Field Guide to Sprawl*

"[Pierson is] a careful observer of the domestic and neighborhood landscapes." —*Book News* (pre-print)

"Melissa Holbrook Pierson's fierce little book channels both
Jane Jacobs and Patti Smith. . . . A haunting meditation on the
loss of cherished places, on dislocated populations, on greed, and
on overdevelopment. . . . [Reading this book] may make you fight
a little harder to save that old building or corner of undeveloped
land down the street from where you live."
—Alan G. Brake, *The Architect's Newspaper*

"The book shows itself to be something more than just a lament
of a lost way of life. . . . Readers will be saddened and outraged at
humanity's obvious shortcomings Pierson lays at our feet, or
swept up in the author's wonderful juxtaposition of her life and
the arc of her argument. . . . Pierson is on to something big and
not often enough discussed." —Todd Peterson, *Pages*

"This is one of those books where an attempt to fold over the corners of pages with memorable quotes and beautiful phrasing has
yielded an immediate dog-eared quality. . . . Pierson's piercing
honesty . . . is distinct and original. . . . Like all great works of
writing, Pierson ends up rendering us a path to redemption."
—Paul Smart, *Woodstock Times*

"A rare gift: It manages to tread the fine line between memoir
and social history with impossible grace. . . . Pierson's work is
rich in detail." —Crispin Kott, *Kingston Times*

"An impassioned meditation on vanishing public and personal
spaces. . . . Pierson writes lushly thoughtful prose. . . . *The Place
You Love Is Gone* makes fresh and powerful the familiar observa-
tion that progress—be it societal or personal—inevitably carries a
price." —Kevin Riordan, *Courier-Post*

MELISSA HOLBROOK PIERSON

THE PLACE YOU LOVE IS

GONE

| PROGRESS HITS HOME |

W. W. NORTON & COMPANY   NEW YORK LONDON

Selections from "The Waste Land" and "Little Gidding" by T. S. Eliot from *Collected Poems 1909–1962*. Used by permission of Faber and Faber Ltd. Excerpt from "Little Gidding" in *Four Quartets*, copyright 1942 by T. S. Eliot and renewed 1970 by Esme Valerie Eliot, reprinted by permission of Harcourt, Inc. "My City Was Gone" Words and Music by Chrissie Hynde © 1982 Clive Banks Music Limited. All Rights Controlled and Administered by EMI April Music Inc. All Rights Reserved. International Copyright Secured. Used by permission. "Bits and Snatches" from *Born To Win* by Woody Guthrie © 1965 (renewed) by Woody Guthrie Publications, Inc. All rights reserved. Used by permission. "Cannonsville" by Stephen G. Pelletier. Originally published in *Kaatskill Life* magazine. Used by permission of the author. "On Cannonsville Reservoir" by Dorothy Kubik. Originally published in *Kaatskill Life* magazine. Used by permission of the author. Unnamed poem, originally published in the *Catskill Mountain News* and collected in *Two Stones for Every Dirt* by Douglas DeNatale. Used by permission of the Delaware County Historical Association and the *Catskill Mountain News*.

Every effort has been made to contact the copyright holders of each of the selections. Rights holders of any selections not credited should contact W. W. Norton & Company, Inc., 500 Fifth Avenue, New York, NY 10110, for a correction to be made in the next reprinting of our work.

Copyright © 2006 by Melissa Holbrook Pierson

For information about permission to reproduce selections from this book, write to Permissions, W. W. Norton & Company, Inc., 500 Fifth Avenue, New York, NY 10110

Manufacturing by Courier Westford
Book design by Judith Stagnitto Abbate
Production manager: Anna Oler

Library of Congress Cataloging-in-Publication Data

Pierson, Melissa Holbrook.
The place you love is gone : progress hits home / Melissa Holbrook Pierson.— 1st ed.
p. cm.
Includes bibliographical references.
ISBN 0-393-05739-9 (hardcover)
1. Progress—Psychological aspects. 2. Real estate development—Psychological aspects.
3. Landscape changes—Psychological aspects. 4. Home—Psychological aspects.
5. City and town life—Psychological aspects. 6. Place (Philosophy) I. Title.
HM891.P54 2005
303.44'0973—dc22

2005024358

ISBN: 978-0-393-32928-5 pbk.

W. W. Norton & Company, Inc., 500 Fifth Avenue, New York, N.Y. 10110
www.wwnorton.com

W. W. Norton & Company Ltd., Castle House, 75/76 Wells Street, London W1T 3QT

1 2 3 4 5 6 7 8 9 0

CONTENTS

To my father,
Charles Pierson,
1922–2003,
and the places he loved

HOME TOWN

I am a fragment, and this is a fragment of me.

—EMERSON, "Experience"

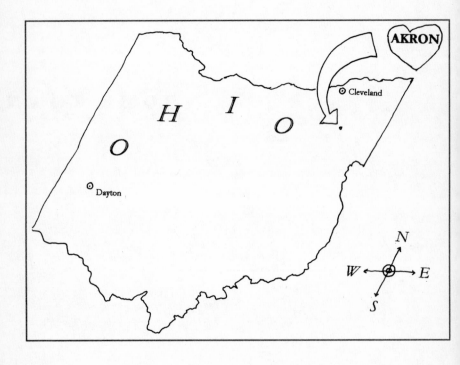

YOU ARE A GIGANTIC, unknowable, towering, tragicomic construction. You can also be traced back to a cell. But this cell needed to meet with bizarre chance so that it was this amoeba (and not that other amoeba) that washed up onshore and started changing shape. Had the weather been slightly different that day, or the sand a tad more wet, the trajectory of the pinball would have been altered by a fraction of a degree. Then it would have banked off the side at a different angle, hit the bumper below the other one, vibrated between bumpers fourteen times instead of twelve with the attendant bells and racking up of points, and finally flushed after one and not two successful applications of the flipper.

For me, that fraction of a degree, hard as it is to grasp, is what was ultimately responsible for the existence of Garner's, a hamburger drive-in on West Market Street. And Garner's is where, in

1954, after some onion rings served in a plastic boat, a certain pleasantly anxious question ("Will you . . .") was posed and breathless answer received. Since that conversation took place between two people who are responsible for making me, as far as I am concerned Garner's is where the world began.

Others think some things obvious, but I have long been prone to marveling. *Odd fluke and inexplicable accident are all that's between you and the hard specificity (the deep red brick of these houses . . . the drive to Skyway in Fairlawn on a spring evening with the windows down) of all that you love.* This is the only reason that Akron, Ohio, is the punch line of a joke to everyone else but to me nothing less than the contents of a secret vault stored deep in the moist center of my soul. Go ahead, then, and laugh, but only if you have never gone down to the Cuyahoga Valley all red-gold in fall, or visited your daddy's office downtown on Main Street in order to feel like the most privileged eight-year-old on earth. Anyone is excused who has not spent moments that turned into weeks that turned into years metabolizing every particle of this hilly green place until it became part of the structure of your skin, bones, teeth. Because no one but the native born can know what it is like to have West Market Street mapped as a straight line through the heart. And it does not matter that West Market Street and its merchants, its old houses and new businesses, stoplights and street signs, are as unremarkable as those on the traversing artery of any medium-sized city in the country, or many other countries. Then again, that both does not matter and it matters a great deal. This is in fact the crux of it all. It has been scientifically corroborated, too. Here's a way-finding study published in 1932, "Spatial Integrations in a Human Maze." Some subjects developed "affection" for landmarks—including a rough board—simply because they were familiar. I think for a moment about an unforgettable piece of wood. Aha! *This* must explain my fondness for Akron.

Somewhere the great theorists of child psychology have isolated the developmental mechanisms that lead to this passing strange love. They have outlined the innate human inclination toward geography, for here the baby traces the map of mother's face with his fingers, over rills and crevasses and seismic disturbances. He feels them with an intensity that does not even recognize their separateness from his own regional being. Somewhere they have written of the grave importance of baby's crib, the bars of which are transformed into a wooden womb beyond the womb. A little later, the circus mobile comes into view and it, too, along with the shadows on the wall and the Little Boy Blue nightlight, are subsumed within the known limits of the world.

How many hours there are to study their mysteries! Colors, beads, light. You have no idea what they really are. Maybe that is why they become impaled on the memory as something incredible. They will be recalled years later with a sharp intake of breath when the little child who has been somehow left to rattle around intact inside the adult suddenly spies some of these inscrutable objects on a return trip home.

One of these eminent men gave it a name: the microsphere. In other words, the repository of *things*. One morning you woke to find that a large rabbit had left something on the dresser in your room. You cautiously approached. At first you could do nothing but stare at this totality of wonders; indeed, staring at it was more delicious than anything else you could possibly conceive of doing with it. A papier-mâché egg gave up its glossy surface to bipedal hares with wheelbarrows and garden tools. Another egg—O bliss untold!—appeared to be frosted like a cake, but it contained a window on a miniature scene inside. The longer you looked, the more you took in of the quality of air and light surrounding the small sugar place you now inhabited, too.

The things you saw became your home. And they became your teachers. They made you an unwitting wizard, an accomplished if pint-sized engineer. Just by looking at them, you caused things to shift shape. After hours of staring at that oxidized-green copper ornament on the roofline of your grandparents' Tudor-style house (your back slightly damp from lying in the shady grass), it revealed itself in certainty: it was a frozen-custard cone. Why would there be ice cream on the roof of a house? Well, to make you look at it in longing, of course.

All the evidence is buried too near the surface, hastily, just a few inches of dirt scratched over the top of the cache. A song is heard distantly on the wind. *Little lunchbox, little lunchbox, little lunchbox o' mine.* Here, the tin barn with thermos silo. There, the pink ballerina. Another, simple and familiar, loved therefore: red plaid. They contain the memory of lunches past—a peculiar smell, of sandwiches curing during the hours between breakfast and noon; long-ago spilled soup and applesauce; the *je ne sais quoi* imparted by wax paper to the whole perfume. How you longed for the Wonder Bread of your mates; how you decried the Pepperidge Farm White of your box. Crusts, begone! Yet, yet . . . sometimes there were Fritos. Years later, the big Time-Life *Picture Cook Book* and its Kodachrome photos of dinner parties circa 1956, barbecues and picnics and "Cooking for Children" (you memorized every chocolate chip and candy apple, the braids on the blue-jeaned girl with her hands full of wet taffy), cause successive frissons to run down your spine with every turn of the page. You must have studied this book with an intensity never rivaled in college art history. You gazed so long into its ravishing pages that you popped out the other side, crouching in the corner of the prairie-style living room in which a dazzling cocktail party was being held, at the exact moment a little boy in sport coat and diminutive bow tie forever reached for a party frank speared through by a toothpick. Or is it simply that the quality of your sight then was that of a different species?

Every one of these things is very, very important, and you have canvassed them all and know them better than any inventor, and still you are only six.

Is it any wonder you grew up to feel murderous, vengeful, toward anyone who would dare change this landscape that made you what you are? "Lost," after all, is a euphemism for "dead." *We lost granny. I have lost everything that I remember.* You may excuse your mother for later wallpapering your room at home, since you may forcibly remind yourself you are well into middle age. But can you forgive the people who, in return for money—nothing but money!—have taken the dirt road upon which you and the salamanders wandered in rich solitude and turned it into Hunter Ridge Estates? The whole thing sticks in your throat. Why, you can't even find it in your heart to look past the absurd overreaching of the name: there never was even a burr-matted Shetland pony in a pen here, much less a barn full of trust-fund horseflesh. The whole thing was begotten in a lie from the get-go. You might have an easier time with it if the salesman's smarm and the builder's pandering, the exclamations and plastic mullions and pretend wrought-iron, had been put down in favor of some concrete-block honesty. You might have an easier time of it if someone would just acknowledge the fundamental existential tragedy of more driveways, of what is lost and how it hurts to know that it will never come back.

In a 1926 German psychology journal the curious case of A. Kirschmann is related. He was born in Oberstein an der Nahe. There, for him, the sun set in the west, and all was well. In 1878 he happened to move to Rippberg. In that place, the sun set in the east. In fact, everywhere Herr Kirschmann went, the sun continued to set in the east. It was only when he got to the embracing vicinity of Oberstein, of home, did the sun change its mind and go where it ought to go. The inner cognitive map by which he oriented himself somehow got flipped when he left his home area. In fact, the whole rest of the world was a disoriented place. *He travels the globe, but only near home does the world right itself.*

Now you are beginning to understand. Frankly, it is a relief to know that your upset has an origin in the dictates of your animal past. Cognitive maps, formed by the brain upon first viewing a place, *really* don't like to be changed, as scientists who study the way we find our way have learned. It is deeply, biologically distressing when a discrepancy between the inner map and reality is discovered. Thus, in a sense, we all truly live in the past—in the map our young minds first made of home.

Losing something dear, as our friends the psychologists also tell us, causes a stoppage at exactly that point. You are stuck at the moment of that loss, a child forever wandering in search of the blue bedroom of home, or like Franco, the man in the Oliver Sacks story who is helpless to do anything but paint perfect replicas of his long-lost home village of Pontito, over and over again, from every possible vantage. You never wanted to be a case for the doctors, but then again, no one ever consulted you when they were making plans to wreck the buildings, widen the streets, level the hills, expunge the vistas, build a basement in your dreams. Your love song has turned into a lament. You can no longer act your age. You lie in the dust of the confusion that has been visited upon your past, and your tears slowly wet the newly poured floor of the SummaCare health center. *O Akron, my Akron, great city of parking decks!*

ALL LOSS IS DRAWN to one vanishing point. It lies on the map at an ostensibly arbitrary place, a dot surrounded by other arbitrary convergences of chance and memory. It is located on the surface of what was left after a particular glacial retreat eons earlier. A certain combination of shale covered by limestone covered by carboniferous conglomerate would result in the kind of accident upon which hopeful industries would be poised. For a moment, though, it was just a rumor carried along Atlantic headwinds to the king of England's court, there to be inked on parchment as real, even if its actual boundaries were uncertain. But the Ohio country would soon become well enough known to whisper its virtues in the ears of people who were willing to struggle across the wilderness from Connecticut to claim them.

Every place writes its own elegy before it is founded. Each beginning is an end to what has preceded it; something has always come before. So excavate your own cellar, then the ruins on top of which it was laid, and the bones beneath the ruins. Then dig some more. I may be a sentimental fool, but I can't deny this particular truth, that it is not so simple as I would like it: paradise is ending on our watch. Then again, it is possible that this is finally true; we shall see, soon. Anyway, I am not fool enough that I would cede my right to complain loudly about what has been stolen from me and no one but me. I take my role as custodian of my nostalgia with a mortal seriousness. Life has supplied me with only these eyes, only this bizarre sensibility composed solely of this accretion of embarrassingly personal, minor events that has solidified into the unshapely mass called "me." None of us lives in the same world. Seven billion planets, not one, currently revolve around the sun in the third place of the solar system. They told you wrong in school. Our personal histories enthrall us, and repel others. Someone else's blather about her family tree or ancient homestead is maddening in exact proportion to her belief in its unique fascination, which is what all people believe about their pasts, definition of "unique" be damned. But find someone who realizes her own bygones are so redundant as to merge with the infinite other droplets into the vast river of human time, and there: now you've got the possibility of a story.

What we are is where we have been. That is all there is, at least from where we can see. They keep trying to convince you that there is some objective reality out there, but you know in your heart how much nonsense that is. It's their way of trying to sell you on the idea that change, being an "inevitable" part of "progress"—being dropped on top of your head by some deus ex machina with a bad sense of timing—can't be fought. You can be choking on it, turning red and beginning to perspire, seeing little things start to float before your eyes, and they'll dismiss you. In fact, they never even bothered to ask. Look in vain for many in-depth studies on the *only thing that matters*, what it feels like to live in the world you live in. That's so they can take your home, the thing that made you, and shatter it, piece by piece.

———

RATTLESNAKES ARE THICK along the way to Sam's Club. An ancient and proud race of native people portages its canoes on the centuries-old path that passes by Broasted Chicken. Wolves dodge six lanes of traffic to cross I-77, trying to reach their fertile suburban hunting grounds recently christened Ridgewood Lakes and adorned with a fountain in a "lake" that attracts many geese.

The hometown of my youth is now recognizable only in the places they haven't got to yet, though I hear plans are afoot. The Akron of my father's youth has left traces, sunken places in the earth, but some of the stories are impossibly quaint. The Akron of his great-great-grandfather Abial, who arrived from Connecticut in the early nineteenth century in a wagon loaded with all his possessions, matters to me only inasmuch as I have a slightly above-average interest in history and an immature tendency to embroider myself into the pictures engraved in books that leave faint sienna stains of disintegrating binding leather on your hands. Otherwise, I bemoan the designation of northeastern Ohio as the Connecticut Western Reserve in the late eighteenth century only because it formed the beginning of what would become my story, and thus contained this terrible drawn-out end of which I am a forced witness. And because on principle one must detest with all one's heart the genocidal greed that brought ruination to civilizations, landscapes, species, and finally papered it over with a likely story of brave pioneer spirit. Yet the years between 1786 and 1957 are mainly of occasional historic, narrative, and detachable aesthetic interest. Certainly, it can be amusing to be reading a book about the Ohio & Erie Canal and come across your forebear's name. But what really matters is the fact that the vistas that made up your very own private wonderful world when you were six are now shards under the foot of the parent company of Bed Bath & Beyond.

At so many points along the way Akron might never have become Akron. It might have clattered like a pebble poised on the ravine's edge that chanced to meet with a traveler's foot. In this it is like everywhere else. In most things it is like everywhere else.

First, as always, there was the matter of the people for whom this was already home, for whom the sight lines and caves and waterways and known places were the mother that made them. To the newcomers these people might as well have been squirrels or wildcats, and can any place be said to belong to them? The only difference was that the people who were here first seemed to require negotiations and treaties; the extirpations were the same. When the foreigners arrived, they keenly appraised the river that for a time was the western boundary of the republic. As usual, "westernmost" was a dubious concept in their minds. Anyway, the river had some falls. This particular place had little else to recommend it, being situated on a relatively unfertile high spot on a continental divide. But a few men had desires that were not to be deterred.

Despite the fact that money was the central sacrament in the rites of the Church of Manifest Destiny, sometimes miscalculations were made. Or perhaps not. The price for the thousand acres from which such raw sentimentality as mine was later to rise was $4.03, in a tax sale. Only by force of imagination (some would go so far as to substitute the word "connivance") of the purchaser and a cohort or two was a "town" brought into being—on paper at least. It always helped to have the scent of classical legend about your enterprise, and so "Akron," Greek for "high place," was stuck to the plat of a nowheresville filed in 1825.

It was not merely coincidental that the canal envisioned by George Washington in 1784 as a way to link the midwest's isolated outposts to the eastern markets was actually begun in 1825 as well. It was to go through the very heart of little Akron. The canal was the town's animating spirit, in the way of those myths of the departed Delawares, Senecas, Wyandots, Chippewas, Ottawas, Mingoes. Life was breathed into a conception, and the requisite tavern and store came into being, along with an attendant population. The ghosts of the former inhabitants moved the air near their former hunting grounds in the valley of the Cuyahoga nearby. A few years later and another commercial idea was enacted, and now the town was to grow to fill the wishful outlines that had been drawn for it; the ghosts were to be neither heard nor felt anymore. A millrace was built to divert water from the Little Cuyahoga down a steep slope through the middle of what was to become a thriving downtown, like a hundred others, and later still a cadaverous downtown, like a thousand others. And that is where a certain native-born sap, a century and a half later, was to come upon its eerie remains. (It is still there, its burbles echoing underneath the Main Street of both snazzy office buildings and cracked storefronts whose boarded doorways are perfumed with antediluvian urine; it still hides there, in a waterless portion amid the weeds of the back end of a forgotten center-town street, plastic bags carried by downpours stretched and caught between rocks.) Perhaps that is why the past exists—to creep out the present. It must take pleasure in the beauty of its strange remnants.

Now young Akron could start on its series of firsts, the coveted world titles that amaze and impress mainly the holder's own populace: the Cereal Capital; the Sewer Pipe Capital; the Clay Marble Capital; the Rubber Capital; all the way to now, when it is the Polymer Capital. These are less apt to excite citizens of other towns only because they, too, have their inevitable claims to industrial fame. Someone has to be Steel City, Bubblegum Capital, Chocolate Town USA. So, for a while, Akron was to be a premier miller of flour. But it really came into its own because a stern German by the name of Ferdinand Schumacher decided to push the issue of rolled oats. The country learned it was more than happy to eat the grain it had formerly fed only to horses. A little while later an impressive army in blue purchased large quantities in its bid to keep the nation together. The German didn't necessarily like losing a more intimate relationship with his grains, but the success of the business made it so top-heavy that he was forced to consolidate and market his product in branded containers bearing the image of a smiling Quaker man.

The turning of mill wheels seems to have scrambled things inside the intellect. Hope—and propaganda—springs eternal.

Anyone who knew Akron a decade after its founding, or a hundred years later, or last week, would have a fine laugh at the words of this anonymous self-appointed lyricist, who in 1835 gave himself leave to envision his burg a full five years in the future:

AKRON IN 1840

The white man came, the savage Indian fled,
The wild-beast started from his leafy bed;
The war-song ended when the mighty blow
Of eastern genius laid the forest low;
Yon rugged hills, that sought the sky in vain,
Fell by the shock, and formed a pleasant plain;
Hence grew this city, which unrivaled stands,
A beacon-light to all benighted lands.

Wishful thinking combined with platitude make for less than great poetry, but you do have to admire the intent. However, even this controlled leap fell short in that our prognosticator was unable to foretell the Panic of 1837, in which only two or three out of a score of stores remained solvent, and real estate bottomed. But the versifier was in the main correct: this city remains unrivaled, because I am the one who now says it, and since I have only one birthplace none other can touch it.

It is impossible for me to say whether rubber has anything to do with it. But a deep thinker would render judgment that Yes! Rubber has everything to do with you, because without the accidents that led to the situating and success in Akron of what were to become the world's great rubber manufacturers—Goodyear, Goodrich, Firestone, General, more than a dozen others—this city would not have gotten past the clay-products stage, and thus your Ohio forebears might have gone to someplace better, like Dayton, and your Greek forebears might never have come to open restaurants in a town without the numerous clientele such a busy industrial center had. And so I hail rubber (though it also forces me to welcome the vandal automobile, which made rubber really take off). I hail the chances taken by the first unsure entrepreneur to locate a plant here in order to produce fire hose decades before the need for tires, and before that the mills that made the place look like a good place to do business, and on back to the canal that made this a place in the first place.

In the five years after 1865, population doubled; it just about did it again between 1890 and 1900. During the decade preceding 1920 it tripled. Around World War I, men outnumbered women by two to one. What an exciting place! Nowhere to sleep! By 1920 Akron was known as "the capital of West Virginia," as so many of the tens of thousands of new rubber workers had followed the beacon-light straight from that benighted land. Among those seeking work and finding it, for a time, was a young Clark Gable. He was one of the faceless masses in the rubber works, as well as in a drugstore and men's furnishings. When he lost those jobs, he went on the road to sell pots and pans; Woody Guthrie would a little later give him appropriate words to sing: "Looky yonder where that fireball's gone! / Goodbye to old Akron goodbye for a while / I'm leaving you now crost many a sad mile." Another who came in the boom years was a strange poet named Hart Crane, who was not like too many others in that he found Akron inspiring material for a poem, albeit a bleak and inscrutable one. It begins, "Greeting the dawn, / A shift of rubber workers presses down / South Main. / With the stubbornness of muddy water" and goes on to call the city "a bunch of smoke-ridden hills." He might have seen some of my relatives, because he noticed that "the dark-skinned Greeks grin at each other."

Culture might have seemed a tough sell in such a place, but America was bubbling over with enthusiastic aspirations. (Oh, where are the hopes of yesteryear?) And since money can buy the fittings of cultural attainment, at least, this is the easiest method for the newly well-to-do to show how thoroughly separated they are from the purposeless accidents that changed their fortunes. This often took the form of mansion building along with celebrity courting. There were dozens of epically scaled houses erected in the decades before and after the turn of the century, sited far enough away from the ill winds blowing past the rubber works downtown. Perhaps you can find some irony in the former Indian trail between important waterways, Portage Path, becoming a favored location, but none was as gobsmacking as Stan Hywet. It was the Tudor-style manor of F. A. Seiberling, founder and president of Goodyear. Not only did it mimic the appearance (and thus morals) of merrie olde feudal England; parts of it were actually shipped to Akron from there. It comprised, and still does, sixty-five rooms, including solarium, Great Hall, music room, billiard room, nursery, bowling alley, swimming pool; it houses twenty-one thousand panes of glass and twenty-three fireplaces. Its outrageous cost may well have contributed to the family's loss of the rubber concern to New York bankers a few years after construction was finished in 1915; but the important thing is that Taft and Hoover, Paderewski, and Helen Keller were guests at the estate, and the money has always been found to keep the slate roof leak free, now out of the pockets of seventy-five thousand paying visitors who arrive each year in minivans by the score and listen to the tour guide with only half an ear since with the rest they are hearing an internal monologue concerning covetousness.

There had been other indications that the amorphous attributes of "culture" were being obtained in the Tip-Top City: theaters, and not only vaudeville; chamber music; institutes of higher learning; lectures. (We proudly recall the time Sojourner Truth came to town many years before to give a little talk that had as its refrain "And ain't I a woman?") It is all right to laugh, but Akron had its own claims to high society, too. It seems not to have always taken itself so seriously, especially as the "prestigious" Portage Hotel downtown sported the Rubber Room lounge, fitted out with appointments of hard rubber; and as an annual event sponsored by the Women's Art League of Akron from 1938 to the next world war was the Rubber Ball, to which celebrants were required to wear rubber costumes. More serious, yet more surpassing strange, was the creation in 1895 of the Akron Golf Club, devoted to golf playing on its three-hole course, at the former home of abolitionist John Brown. In 1922 the club (since relocated, given more holes, and renamed the Portage Country Club) rebuilt after a fire, and the architectural style chosen was . . . Tudor Revival. Whole chunks of Akron had been done up in brick and half-timber during the teens. It is interesting to note that the vogue for an architecture that referred to the intensively hand-built and agrarian occurred during an unprecedented expansion of modern technology. The "Wedding of the Century," between Martha Firestone and William Clay Ford—their families' chief products had already been long married on the roads of America—occurred in 1947 at Harbel Manor, the bride's grandfather's Akron estate. It was Tudor.

These things that happened years ago and that don't matter to anyone are long-gone wind and rain. Ephemeral, meaningless. But they amount to forces that shaped the rocky earth and waterways (the buildings and institutions and beliefs and histories) that made me. Guard against its theft, the past of the place that made you. At least notice it, if you cannot save it.

A WRITER FOR *The American Mercury* wrote of the varied fortunes of this fine metropolis in 1926:

> Akron is truly the rubber city. It blew itself up, burst, fell flat, and rose again; sadder and wiser, of course, but optimistic, aggressive—and still unbeautiful.

But what Akron could he be talking about? The quadrants of all existence in this place were ever beautiful. In the darkening twilight we were still playing kick the can in the deep yards before the gracious Tudor houses. The street lamps began glowing by magic, yellow acorns of milk glass atop green fluted poles, as the sun disappeared. The sidewalks hosted our bicycle races down gentle slopes, with sudden veerings for those well-anticipated four-inch bumps caused by the roots heaving up from the great old trees that marched down the devil strip. (In Ohio we had our own nomenclature, which some assumed was the lingua franca of the world until learning different when out of state at college; this was the case with "parmas," the word for nerdy white socks, meanly named after the Cleveland suburb with a large population of Polish immigrants.) No power lines uglied the streetscape, since they were buried underground by decree of P. W. Litchfield. He was another of those who found rubber manufacturing akin to money manufacturing. Later president of Goodyear, he laid out the neighborhood at the same time he planned his own great house, the Anchorage. It was down at the end of our street. Take a left and go up a small hill from there, and you'd run into the carriage house of Stan Hywet. In fact we often did. Our mothers might caution us to be careful in crossing Portage Path, the great thoroughfare of rushing traffic through our little world of beautiful Akron, or then again they might not. We have forgotten that it barely had any traffic then. They might also not even know where we were from nine in the morning until dinner. But Stan Hywet had magnetic lures: it was largely devoid of people over all its hundred acres of generally overgrown grounds, and it sold candy sticks and seductive miniature glass animals in its gift shop. The past came to haunt the present on these grounds; we were being touched by icy fingers and grew to develop a taste for it. Ruin and decay were breathed in by tender nostrils until they became the faded perfume on mother's best coat. Wander until you find the ghost of the old grass tennis court; erect a net in your mind between the rusty posts, and a fence to connect the four metal poles at the corners, and then stand on the back line until you can hear the thwack of the ball being hit through an octave of girlish laughter. The sun will always be dappled through the trees. Run the bridle paths through the woods as if you were a horse (you are). Sit by the pool of the English garden, the secret garden sunk behind high walls and now your own. Imagine your wedding at the end of the birch allée progressing from the side porch all the way to a plashing fountain (broken) and a vantage from a balustrade overlooking a lake (now swamp), on the banks of which peacocks once roamed. Because it was possible to be "known" in this small formerly great world, you could be admitted to the house without having to endure for the dozenth time the tour guide's description of how the dumbwaiter and the house telephone worked, or of the provenance of the acre-sized oriental rug that would be rolled up by a squadron of servants in formation prior to a ball. At one point there would be a children's art class, and during its assignment time you would always choose the brown-tiled solarium, with its niche fountain echoing the brief splash of water into the room for your ears alone, to which to retire with your sketch pad. It really became your room, as you rarely saw anyone else in it. Your imagination inhabited it, and this house, and so the child acts as god, conceiving and animating the world in his week's work. Then the child grows, only to find his beloved creation quietly pried from his hand while he slept. It is spiffed up, others invited to take it over and do what they will with it (usually involving large fees). Is it any wonder he reviles the rules made necessary by huge clots of new population—*I'm sorry, we do not allow departures from the tour; welcome to the newly refurbished Japanese Garden: be respectful of others' peace and quiet in this special place*—and finds a hole burned through his heart?

Is THIS WHERE it all begins—all life, love? And finally where reside the remains of both when the years have rolled persistently over the mountains of experience and finally crushed them to a moraine of uniform gravel? In the left medial temporal lobe?

They have identified the loci of the mystical creation of you: posterior parahippocampal gyrus; hippocampus; anterior parahippocampal gyrus; little spots in the gray extrusions coiling around the MTL. The contents of your mother's jewelry drawer, first furtively explored when you were five, stored here forever. So, too, the smell rising up from the plastic plates and cups in the heat of the sun in grandma's side yard as you played tea party with your cousins under the rose arbor, lo these many decades ago. There is no comprehending why certain sights are returned while others go—no, it doesn't make sense that you still can remember in detail the look of another child's brown shoes under the bathroom-stall door in kindergarten, yet not the face of the teacher—but your mind is a strange album full of what they call flashbulb memories, images printed on a chemically sensitive brain by a sudden shock of light. Thus you recall where you were standing in the living room within range of the walnut hi-fi announcing urgent news of a president's violent death—not because this news stunned you but because your mother's reaction did. Her stricken expression was the light that momentarily blinded you, leaving yellow blankness where the world should be, the quick blinking finally bringing a gray shape into existence on top of that lemony background: the frozen image in negative of her face.

You are a repository of memories and little else. They are everything to you. Some people have no respect for them. They do not care if they are what keep you alive—yes, literally. Ask Mr. Shaw, the Welsh banker kidnapped recently in Tbilisi, Georgia, and kept chained by the neck in an underground hole for four months. An account of his ordeal notes that "in order to survive captivity, he had summoned up memories from his childhood."

You hear the echo in that, right? You hear the distant ringing of the school bell, though there never was a school bell in your day anyway. You hear a thousand poems as through a wall, you hear the ancients and the moderns, as there never was a man of thought who did not feel this particular deep and provocative melancholy. You hear above all (far, far above all) the voice of impossible beauty, the author of Sonnet XXX:

> *When to the sessions of sweet silent thought*
> *I summon up remembrance of things past . . .*

He has given a title to some translators of what could be said to be the last word on the criticality of memory ("final word" comprising 2,259 pages of final words, give or take) to the experience of life: an anti-epic of epic proportions that is the bible of all those who believe small details to be quite big enough. Anyone who does not understand how a soggy madeleine can do as much as Heinrich Schliemann in excavating lost worlds does not deserve the richness of his own history. For he would not understand how there is really no difference between a scent caught by accident and the sudden comprehension of all mortality; no difference between a color seen smeared on distant hills by autumn trees and the realization that discontinuity is continuous in life, and just how pleasantly strange it all is. Such a one could not appreciate the blurring of genres that is the true expression of experience—he would have to keep asking himself if Proust really remembered all this from his own childhood, or did he invent a character who related an invented past (as if that distinction ever mattered)—and could not get the fact that the book he holds in his hand is the book that is being discussed in the book as a *postulated* book. Thus he wouldn't get the whole bloody point about a book that asks whether a book can encapsulate time's passage through a life while it does just that. And so the whole question of what genre it belongs to, and whether it is "fact" or "fiction," is ambushed and left by the side of the road for dead.

As one reads the terribly French book, one might be surprised to hear some music in the background and note that it is a musical score by the terribly American Aaron Copland. It arises because he, too, is a poet of pure yearning. The music is at once lonely and comforting, full of longing for what we have and what we must do without. He is not thinking high thoughts, as Ives does; he is channeling love in a half sob for places, these views down dirt roads on quiet days, strangers passing by in the establishing shot of an old black-and-white movie set in a small town of simple houses and three-story brick buildings on a Main Street that was even then fading into oblivion. This is what *ache* sounds like. And so I think of home when I hear it; or of Home. North-eastern Ohio on a dry day in fall, sitting on its map of the heartland, within the embrace of an America that never was. It is a supremely consoling abstraction—noble aspirations, good, simple people, stern religion but hope, always hope—that rises out of *Appalachian Spring* or *Music for Movies* ("New England Countryside," "Barley Wagons," "Sunday Traffic," "Grovers Corners," "Threshing Machines") like a spirit vapor. And you need a librettist for this opera of personal nostalgia: naturally, Robert Frost has volunteered for the job. He might have written in the first decades of the twentieth century, that age of our grandmothers' timeless houses and the moment of which we most decry the destruction, but he, too, was weeping over loss! This should make us think a moment, but we are on a roll. He views decay and finds it ripe. He looks over the American land to find "The woods come back to the mowing field," over and over. He sees that the place he inhabits is gone even as he speaks of gone: this was a world where ruin and forgottenness had their purpose ("I dwell in a lonely house I know / That vanished many a summer ago"). Imagine an *abandoned farm* in New England now. The formaldehyde has barely been pumped into the empty veins of the owner before the real-estate brokers have the executor on speed dial.

The very idea! If it is suggestively rotting, now its cracked paint will be expertly (but not too expertly) replicated for sale in the kind of store that is safe for the buyer who could never bring herself to go where she might encounter *the original* suggestively rotting piece. If a place is genuinely decomposing and lonely, its fate is to be made splinters beneath the Caterpillar's tracks. Intimations of mortality, dark places to discover upon parting the thick weave of wild grape: no more. No time for that.

What is lost? Just some lovely loneliness, some fruitful yearning. Something that can be yours alone. The past leaching its dyes into the present. Witness of continuity. Possession of what extends beyond your body and its eyes, creation of understanding. Your interior life coming to shake hands in happy greeting with the sender of the anonymous checks that have kept it alive all along. Home. The widening circle around your astonished gaze.

Home is your mother. She made you; you and she are bonded by blood and smell, by the cells that over years have sloughed off your being and that now lie inches thick on her floors. It has been observed that it is the nonliterate who become most attached to their homes: the Australian aborigines, the American Indians who wasted away in grief when forced to leave the places they had inhabited since prehistory. And who is a nonliterate if not a child? He is the quivering, watchful deer. He does not dilute his experience by thinking about it: it floats directly into his being via a sharp breeze, the coolness on his skin carrying a scent to his nose and a dryness to his tongue that he immediately associates with the sound of leaves scudding by, vision pulled cloudward. And so forth.

Change is a violation of personal laws. Change is an essential character of everything in this world. The nutcracker has your head in its grip. Time ratchets down the screw. Your most primitive desires are impossible to deny, impossible to fulfill. Your kvetching is grounded and groundless. And "progress" is the Mother Goose you were raised on, until you grew up and learned the bloody history behind the happy rhymes and could never hear them again without thinking of blackness and betrayal.

A truism is here repeated for the first time: "Since consciousness lies in the individual, an egocentric structuring of the world is inescapable." This is the formulation of Yi-Fu Tuan, a geographer and woefully underread writer, in *Topophilia*, a mesmerizingly successful attempt to define "all the different ways that human beings can develop a love of place." Incredible, then, that rarely has anyone sought to survey or scientifically observe *what people see in or feel about the man-made environment in which they live*. Billions of dollars have been spent to, say, torture animals to death with chemicals, so that we know, to no real end, the precise amount that will be lethal to exactly 50 percent of the test dogs. (Go ahead, check the insert in your prescription vaginal-yeast cream, and look for "LD-50.") But barely one cent to understand the origin of your love. It is no wonder, then, that with no one paying attention, we could be so utterly snookered that we have sold our birthright to the devil in exchange for a wide selection of bath mats.

Did you catch that scent? The one that sends you tumbling back through the years and pulls aside the curtain on an entire scene of youth: cut grass and suddenly it's July thirty-seven years before, and you see the holes in your father's tennis shoes and remember exactly how the driveway's white gravel hurt your bare feet; a certain hot odor that you much later pinned to an unnamed summer-blooming bush instantly brings back the feel of sweat prickling your neck as you pull a wagon down the piping hot concrete-and-sand path from the food store on Fire Island. Of course, science once again explains it all, and as usual the truth is as fully poetic as the phenomenon it accounts for. The cortex, where memories are stored, evolved from the little nut of the primitive brain devoted to smell. They say that if you really want full recall of that once-in-a-lifetime trip to the Far East, wear a new cologne. Then go home and wait a year or two to take it from the cabinet again. One sniff and you're back in the countryside, marveling over the distant view of an ancient pagoda.

But it's the recollection of those childhood smells and sights that really gets you. They have an edge, a vibrancy that makes you wonder if maybe you really died some years ago and now just wander your world as a ghost with no nose. Nothing can approach them; they are just like life! They define life! But of course: the child is closer to the ground by a few feet, closer to all perfumes that emanate from the earth. And his senses are not yet ground down by age. His taste buds are still there on the hard and soft palate, the sides of the throat and the upper tongue, while yours have now retreated from there. He still sees with the whole of his vision, but you now look with the peripheral receptors. You are no longer seeing the full spectrum of color, either, because the violet end is harder to discern. Your hearing at high frequencies is dulled to almost half that of the child. You no longer explore the world by feeling it all at once, scrambling and falling and jumping and touching. And here's the thing: you no longer experience anything for the first time. That was the real juju. As a child you simply did not wear the fuzzy gloves of received wisdom that prevent the true feel of an object under your fingers. Then, there was no explaining, just absorption.

What was it that seeped into your skin day and night, right into those powerful senses that were busy as a machine, pumping to make raw material into the memories that later sent you reeling when they chanced to knock you on the head? It was your home. Your house, the first place that claimed you.

> And after we are in the new house, when memories of other places we have lived in come back to us, we travel to the land of Motionless Childhood, motionless the way all Immemorial things are. . . .

> Memories of the outside world will never have the same tonality as those of home and, by recalling these memories, we add to our store of dreams; we are never real historians, but always near poets, and our emotion is perhaps nothing but an expression of a poetry that was lost.

A whole book devoted to my subject! Gaston Bachelard, *The Poetics of Space*, published in 1958, no doubt written in part in 1957, the year in which I gestated, too. (There must have been something in the air, something that made one especially permeable.) I could quote the whole thing, but I need to keep my job. So just one more:

> Among the most difficult memories, well beyond any geometry that can be drawn, we must recapture the qual-

ity of the light; then come the sweet smells that linger in the empty rooms, setting an aerial seal on each room in the house of memory. Still farther it is possible to recover not merely the timbre of the voices, "the inflections of beloved voices now silent," but also the resonance of each room in the sound house. In this extreme tenuousness of memory, only poets may be expected to furnish us with documents of a subtly psychological nature.

The philosopher needs to call upon the poet; he can't get all the way down to the basement of this experience by himself. But he says what it's really all about: loss. Impending loss. Knowing for sure that loss is coming and prophylactically mourning it. (*A poetry that was lost; "beloved voices now silent."*) Man, I was anticipating it from way before I knew what it meant.

Every theft engenders anger in the victim. Henry James knew how to get angry. He returned to the United States in 1904 after nearly thirty years abroad. What he sees flummoxes him, deeply dismays him. He uses pages of *The American Scene* to fulminate against the new show of wealth in houses "and their candid look of having cost as much as they know how," which "would have cost still more had the way been shown them." He rails against the insensible greed evinced by the new "sky-scraper." But most of all he laments—nay, has a tantrum over—the change brought to his Greenwich Village home, the lockbox of memory: "There, I repeat, was the delicacy, there the mystery, there the wonder, in especial, of the unquenchable intensity of the impressions received in childhood. They are made then once for all, be their intrinsic beauty, interest, importance, small or great; the stamp is indelible and never wholly fades."

These were the felicities of the backward reach, which, however, had also its melancholy checks and snubs; nowhere quite so sharp as in presence, so to speak, of the rudely, the ruthlessly suppressed birth-house on the other side of the Square. That was where the pretence that nearly nothing was changed had most to come in; for a high, square, impersonal structure, proclaiming its lack of interest with a crudity all its own, so blocks, at the right moment for its own success, the view of the past, that the effect for me, in Washington Place, was of having been amputated of half my history.

He would go out and fight, too, if only the cowards who had done that had stayed hanging about the fountain or the arch. We would all fight: what immorality, what greed, what injustice. But of course we can't find the enemy, and our wild swing of a left hook meets air and makes us spin once and a half around, tangling our legs to the ground. Even through our humiliated tears, we see a small suspicion scuttle across our sight. God, how we hate that. But there it is: the feeling that it is not as simple as that, an enemy and us, a robber and the robbed. "James cherished the landscape he remembered [writes historian John R. Stilgoe in *Common Landscape of America, 1580 to 1845*], and used his memories as the standards by which he condemned the new scene and the social and economic forces it objectified. But the changes that took such stark and sometimes sinister form at the close of the nineteenth century began in James's boyhood, or even earlier." While we were enjoying the beautiful unimportant moments that were later to be all-important, the ground beneath our feet was massing for the earthquake that was to swallow them. Perhaps the children of Ohio's northeastern grasslands were equally unheeding on a warm spring day in 1825, when they paid no mind to the talk about the new Erie Canal because they were too engrossed in feeling the new calves tickle their hands with their sandpaper tongues. Soon most of those cattle would be no more, as the canal would change farming practices in a large part of the state when it opened those eastern markets for grain.

So who to blame for the elevation of the Destroyer Car—the first enemy that comes to hand for anyone of age in this age—to godhead: the tire and automobile industry that together sat on top of public transport until it expired; the Eisenhower administration's addiction to highways; subsidies or zoning and building codes or things that happened to cities in the thirties or our whole damn history moving, moving like a stream that can't be stopped?

Somehow you knew it would all be lost, anyhow. You knew it in your dreams; they left a sad residue, and you saw yourself again running in a well-lit darkness (saw yourself and were yourself at once, the peculiar gift of dreams) over the lawns of your first neighborhood on Halloween night. If it hadn't wanted to tell you something about loss, it wouldn't have recurred several times, until you were both afraid to fall asleep lest it appear again like the compulsion that grew into a monster and eager to welcome it back like an old friend.

Wait; how was it that Walt Disney got to place *his* childhood under glass? (Even as he was part of the larger force that wrecked it.) He based his amusement park's "Main Street U.S.A." on the Main Street of Marceline, Missouri, where he grew up. Of course, he prettied it up a bit, but isn't that what memory does? As James Howard Kunstler points out with customarily eloquent and appropriate indignation in *The Geography of Nowhere*, Henry Ford, too, had the money to do what anyone else can only daydream about: make his childhood come alive again. He built Greenfield Village in Dearborn, Michigan, as a replica of life in the 1880s—his own youth. He did it by buying up the boyhood houses of his personal heroes: the Wright Brothers, Harvey Firestone, H. J. Heinz. And what did he re-create? The very world the automobile helped destroy.

"A MAN IS but what he knoweth," saith Francis Bacon. We have entered an age in which it is nothing to lose the template upon which our beautiful specificity is based, the mold into which we were poured as protoplasm and emerged as something solid, indented with its marks. The Bororo Indians of Brazil arranged their huts in a large circle, facing in. When they were forced by missionaries (oh, save us!) to resituate their shelters in other patterns, nothing less than their entire worldview and self-image went up like smoke.

WITH NO PAST, you can imagine no future. The path that winds you-know-not-where into the world begins in your childhood home; it is located both in space and in time, and everything unspools from its center.

> Each [medieval landschaft] was for its inhabitants a rep-
> resentation of the world because each was the world. . . . If
> they did travel they usually visited a contiguous landschaft
> much like their own but for them lacking the richness of
> association to which they were accustomed. At home
> every spot was invested with meaning—the meadow where
> someone saw the Devil at the edge of the forest, the
> houses of the well-off and the hovels of the poor, the hill
> struck twice by lightning long ago.
>
> —JOHN R. STILGOE, *Common Landscape of*
> *America, 1580 to 1845*

What you have perceived is what shapes the universe. It is what has shaped you, you will realize with justified awe, if only you will go back to wander in the old orchards of childhood, now gone in ugliness and for personal gain, and feel the wretched anger of this loss.

About these things that have such boundless consequence—no one ever asks anybody. No one gets a vote. "Yep, they're paving over that landscape that's as much a part of me as my arm. Sure wish it weren't happening. . . ." They change everything (thus a

retroactive version of *you*), and they didn't *even ask if they could.*
The bastards.

FIVE MINUTES FROM HOME and we're driving into the Cuyahoga Valley. From here, I can see that I am driving back years and
years, back into childhood, for all that I describe is gone now, or
almost all. At the cross of the railroad tracks there is a gas station
and a few shops. At another crossroads a half mile later, where
one road arches back up the steep hill toward the town of Cuyahoga Falls, there is a dark little roadhouse called the Lodge, which
serves a couple different forms of beef. Then the pavement goes
along the banks, and winds under trees, or straightens out past
the old farms. One of them is where we pick our Halloween
pumpkins, after sitting to be photographed on a small mountain
of them in the back of a wagon. The memory struggles under an
equal heap of lacerating nostalgia. We simply called this place
"the valley," because we knew in some well-obscured part of us
that the Cuyahoga was the origin of everything. Not only was it
primal in itself, a slow meandering of brown water through quiet
brown woods, but we would not be here except for it. We barely
notice its existence.

The sound track to life in the dark hours is the whistle of the
freight train that goes by the valley a half mile from our house.
The sound calls up a chorus of weeping. Long ago I seem to have
believed it was a vestige of some parallel world in which lonely
people rode forever through the night toward unknowable desti-
nations. Later I came to know that this is true.

Downtown is just that: a descent along West Market Street to
a toy town graspable in its entirety from a quarter mile away. Skyscrapers—why, Akron has 'em! The First National tower (twenty-
eight stories high!), the art deco YMCA, the sixties racy
black-glass rectangle rising above Cascade Plaza. If I could have
just prevented the car at the crest of Market from making its

majestic roll toward destiny in the form of this midwestern Oz, perhaps I could have watched the magical resetting of the back-drops in the shadow box: a card removed from the back shifts the scene slightly, replacing the Akron that had stood still for my grandparents with the one that had done the same for my father. The changes are subtle, not that I care. Anything that was still there in 1965 from any earlier era must stay; anything gone before then was gone without notice by me. O'Neil's department store lay over the ruins of the Merrill pottery works, but the miracle of the mechanized Christmas windows and their tinselly promise are the only losses at that spot which I can shed a tear for. My father's tears were his and his alone.

Going downtown was a rare and special treat. Mainly we stayed in our small snow globe of suburban happiness, venturing out most often toward the civilities of little adjunct Fairlawn, to Bisson's grocery store or to the Fairlawn Shopping Plaza, the Swim and Tennis club, or along the way to Swenson's drive-in or the depressing gloom of grandma's apartment in the twenties Twin Oaks Apartments or around the corner from there to the library at Highland Square. Going downtown meant visiting Daddy, which was serious business, his office as weighty with silence as a temple. It might also mean going with my mother to classes at the Art Institute, in the former Carnegie library every burg was blessed with, to be inducted into the mysteries, the transporting odors, of paints. Easter at the University Club and Thanksgiving at the Akron City Club, perched atop the Ohio Building, its white tablecloths and our white gloves and white socks under black patent-leather shoes. It was a downtown blown into the air to be caught on a high wire, teetering with the wind forward into the new age of superfluous downtowns and backward into the great bustling heyday of those vital decades in the first half of the twentieth century. It was the downtown of the elemental midwestern city, with its pretensions and strivings, its vigor and crudeness, fictively described in a no doubt equally expendable 1957 novel by Otis Carney called *When the Bough Breaks*:

Six hundred and sixty miles southeast of Minneapolis lay another city, larger, smokier, a city of foundries, rubber manufacture, chemical plants. And if Minneapolis could be called the western outpost of the Middle West, this city was the eastern. It lay in the Saugano River Valley of central Ohio; more accurately, it plugged the south end. . . . What had once been Saugano Marsh was now a sprawling industrial development, perhaps the largest in the Midwest outside of Chicago. Here were the vast plants of U.S. Steel, Goodyear, Du Pont, International Harvester; here too rose the home stacks of such powerful enterprises as Dennison Machine Tool, Achilles Brass and Monarch Corporation.

A half mile to the north was the city's downtown district, known as the Bend, owing to the river's topography at this point. . . . The Bend had its streetcars, its New York Central and B&O terminal; it had, too, the older, more revered institutions like the *Scimitar*, Ohio's only newspaper still in its founding family's hands; and the Ohio Club, even a shade more exclusive than the best suburban club, the Valley Hunt and Field.

But wait. This sounds more like Cleveland, that towering eminence thirty miles to the north, situated on the wide mouth of the Cuyahoga where it joins the gray vastness of Lake Erie. A relation of mine recently remarked, in explanation of some phenomenon or other, "Well, Akron has always had a bit of a complex, you know, being in the shadow of Cleveland." This he said with a straight face, because it is the sad truth to those whose feet feel steady only when upon the solid soil of Akron. By anyone anywhere else, this would be delivered with the hyperbolic raised eyebrows and curling sneer of a comedy club's stand-up.

Aw, what did we need with *Cleveland*? Sure, we went there on exciting trips, to the lakeshore sometimes, more often to shop in aforementioned white gloves and plaid coats the fine establishments of Terminal Tower or Shaker Square. (It was sadly not possible to find Pappagallo shoes in Akron.) The place frightened me. It was too big. No, the frisson of my hometown was quite enough. It did not have to be delivered from outside; it grew from within. I felt the same reverberation in my center that was emanating from the sights along its streets, and we were one. We had two department stores, not six, but the sight of O'Neil's and Polsky's sitting across from each other on corners of South Main like battlements on a border was almost thrilling. We had history—and purchases— there. Grandmother Russell (née Kalafates, married to a man né Roussinos) was well-known by all the salesladies in O'Neil's and was a regular in the Topaz Room, the sanctum sanctorum for the fashionable Akronite. Her husband was the proprietor of the London House—previously known as the Beefeater until a letter was received from the legal counsel of the liquor concern—but he had his own string of lost places unreeling behind him: the La Paix, and before that the Roxy Café, opened with uncanny timing at the outset of the Depression, ornate and orderly and devoid of customers in the promotional portrait taken by Stivas Studios, since the Greeks always patronized the Greeks.

Others' history, too, flowed along the arteries of this town, and my blood joined the river of theirs as I encountered these places. Look: the Planters peanut and confectionery store outside which a bespectacled legume had motioned to many decades of Main Street passersby, though I thought only to me. And see there the Civic Theater, a Loews (its twin separated at birth and laid down in New York City's borough of Queens) opened in 1929 and intended to resemble "a night in a Moorish garden" replete with clouds that moved over a starlit sky of a ceiling. I took full possession of the place and banished all others the first night I attended. The endless depth of intimation behind the statues, waiting to come to life inside their niches bathed in gold light, was enough to make me dizzy. These were part of the Akron of my father's youth, and when I took them, too, he further became part of me. If only I could have walked by the Quaker Oats plant on my way from my home on Fir Hill toward the heart of downtown and stopped to watch the hulls of newly puffed grain ("shot from cannons!") float in the air like snow as they were rhythmically expelled between the cracks of the massive stones in the foundation. This was his memory, though my dreams have commandeered it. It now ricochets in the hollows of my head between the reality of my own youth—the oats silos turned into hotel rooms and the factory into shoppes—and my borrowed memories of his youth, in a time when such commercial quotation of prior life in order to sell things to the nostalgia set had not yet been conceived.

I can't help it if I want to live in the past! It's *my* past, the time forty years ago when there was still some wide-open space into which to insert some dreaming, and still some darkness at night over it. There was quiet, the birthright of all us animals, and somehow there was more time in a day than there is now, and the sole thing you can find to explain that is that there were fewer damn people. What will we do in another twenty years, when another hundred million squalling infants have taken their rightful place as consumers with a desire to consume at all costs? Have no time left to breathe?

The nostalgists are bravely marching into battle, eager to face the advancing tanks of human history. Our hearts are filled with the strength of righteousness. We take up arms in readiness: our plastic cocktail swords glint green and red in the sun. The war correspondent's reports to the homefront make you laugh at our fatal narcissism. *Don't you know that you can't win against the Way Things Have Always Been? And why would you even want to, you pathetic excuse for an army?* We are trying to be what we are not: every other species that has inhabited the same ecological niche for hundreds of thousands of years without the need for an eight-bedroom house where three used to do. We alone do not emit those mysterious pheromones that slow procreation when the carrying capacity of the land has been reached. Our neural pathways were formed by millions of years of existence in communities of our fellows where daily congregation and rituals and exercises made us what we became, and thus whole. Then a few years ago, give or take, they thought up the fetishization of personal property and the automobile and the installation of industry at the tippytop of the rights chain, and bingo: no more meeting places and no more walking and no more breathing of air and viewing of sky and mythmaking to explain the experience. Now you drive to a slushy parking lot and gingerly step into Walgreens for a newspaper and some Rolaids and quickly back the car out after assuring the concerned clerk (he asked, after all) that you're fine today and equally concerned about his psychic well-being (you asked, after all). You then leave the site of what was formerly a heavily used sidewalk in front of a bank, a café, and a shoe store that your grandparents, lacking a car but living nearby, used to walk to. Invisible hands reached down and changed it all around like chess pieces, and you don't know whom to bite. No one else seems to have noticed.

Sometime in the mid-seventies the old orchard around the corner that had been there since the Civil War and where we used to play softball became the yard of a mansard-roofed mansionette. It was the last piece of common ground in the neighborhood, after they made Stan Hywet a showpiece and fixed the holes in the fencing. The dirt road in the very old village in which was located the boarding school near Akron I went to in 1972, down which I would wander without seeing a soul and practice exceedingly bad art photography on an abandoned cottage, was paved in the early eighties. Now cars can drive adequately fast to the million-dollar suburban châteaux that grace every last lot in the expensively quaint town.

The canal that made Akron died officially in 1913, when a serious flood called for the emergency dynamiting of some locks, but it had actually been dispatched to whatever heaven expired transportation systems go to at least twenty-five years before that. Railroads had made canals obsolete.

The 1951 *Hammond's City Street Map Atlas and Trip Guide*, conveniently sized for the briefcase of the commercial traveler—

"Even the purchase of 78 separate city maps and a library of large-volume guides and transportation books, would not enable the user to assemble such a wealth of pertinent information"—contains Akron on its first page. (The next page is Albany, and the last is Worcester, Massachusetts, so there you go.) In addition to arriving on any of the four defunct airlines serving it via its defunct municipal airport, one could alight at the bus station, now a ghost, from a seat on an A&M, Transit, Blue Ridge, Burlington-American, or Greyhound coach. We won't even discuss the five train lines. Likewise the lodgings downtown (*"See map for additional hotels"*). The book is a Ouija board to the spirit world.

The Western Fruit Basket, downtown, was owned by Greeks. That's where we could get the makings for our taramasalata, our olives in jars with brine, our grape leaves, our olive oil. The folks at Bisson's would have been alarmed. Akron preferred its food with a white accent or, if colored, primary, like in Lucky Charms. So Bisson's is where we got the ingredients for our New England boiled dinners and our Hellmann's mayonnaise (the best, mother insisted). On special days Daddy brought home Hough bakery's frosted brownies and was fortunate if he got one himself, since he always waited until well after his martini and dry-roasted peanuts, which in our house was too late. It might have been a bakery, but I don't think they made bread there, much less organic spelt-millet, not to mention sundried tomato focaccia. Bread came presliced in packages at the grocery, and you marked yourself suspicious by picking up a loaf of Pepperidge Farm.

One night not so long ago at Beau's, which until recently occupied a space in Fairlawn Plaza a few doors away from what was the doomed Bisson's second (and only) branch, the specials on the menu included an appetizer of beef carpaccio on arugula with capers, romano, red onion, and olive oil. For dinner one might flag the waiter and request grilled swordfish with roasted tomato and kalamata-olive salsa over spinach, topped with a balsamic drizzle. Also dining there you would encounter the other neighbors whose tastes have lately risen beyond the ability of the chef at

Portage Country Club to satisfy, and who may or may not be talking about the wines they had on their last trip to Paris.

Until 1965, Fairlawn Plaza was about the only place other than downtown to go shopping. We didn't know we needed anything else. Then the mall opened, another half mile down West Market Street. Why the Summit Mall was such a superior experience that soon no one wanted to shop downtown was not revealed to those of us with average brains. But it so clearly was. The apogee of vendibles had been reached. It was not given to us to imagine any needs not yet met by the gleaming corridors and looming anchor stores of this great mercantile presence on the outskirts of town. To do so would have been to look beyond toward blank skies over flat farmland.

Oh, all right. Not completely blank: man had installed a stand named the Freeze, so that the Little Leaguers could salve their bruised egos with postgame frozen custard, and the Putt-R-Golf course (1952) and a drive-in movie theater (1948). And *then* blank skies over flat farmland. It was beautiful.

Sometime in the mid-fifties the oldest story was played out again, yet again, to two people who were unimportant or else who comprised everything, depending. As the egg split, split once more, grew in its inexorable way toward Melissahood, other things were happening. Many, many other things, but you can take just one: the highway system. Yes, the interstates were fluttering down through space, landing on the earth like black ribbons dropped from the clouds. Who could have guessed what this simple act would bring into being? Very weird to stare at the pictures: earthmovers, Caterpillar tracks, yellow-helmeted anonyms of large-scale construction; the dirt contoured to the horizon in expressive whorls and at the edge a tree or two—whatever are they doing there? Weird, because henceforth the eye can no longer accept anything but this, as if the construction occurred primarily in the cortical receptors. Concrete was poured, and concrete it has been for all time.

The area was known as Montrose. In 1973 I-77 was chanced

to be connected to State Route 21, and the minds of men were turning, turning. "There was nothing there. It was empty," explained one of these forward thinkers to the newspaper with pride. Empty—just space, grass, nothing that people could buy. Three hundred and sixty acres of uselessness. Then, in something like six days, the world was created. Between 1970 and 1990, business square feet—planned, approved, built—in Montrose rose from one hundred thousand to about five and a half million. The forecast for the end of the first decade of this century is another three and a half million. ("Corporations have neither bodies to be punished, nor souls to be condemned, they therefore do as they like": Edward Thurlow, Lord Chancellor, 1731–1806.) Into being from clay, fully formed, sprang West Market Plaza, Rosemont Commons—appropriate home for that perfect manifestation of the commons ideal, the community Wal-Mart—Shops of Fairlawn, Builders Square, and Market Square, shopping centers built behind shopping centers, Sam's Club, Bed Bath & Beyond, Super Kmart, Cost Plus World Market (indeed), Cellular One, Pier 1, Border's, T.J. Maxx, MC Sporting Goods, Old Navy, Pet Fair, CompUSA, Sears, The Home Depot, Taco Bell, Chipotle, Red Lobster, Romano's Macaroni Grill, Cracker Barrel, Boston Market, Bob Evans, Ruby Tuesday, Friendly's, Baja Fresh, more and more and more until you fall, sated, heart bleeping faintly, unconscious of the sky above or the ground below or whatever could matter except crawling back to the Camry and waiting for the bank of lights at Cleveland-Massillon Road to give you a left arrow so you can creep home along West Market, finally to transport the contents of two dozen plastic bags into the house which will, somehow, absorb it all.

It is no longer possible to imagine what this place looked like as fallow fields with a slightly leaning white house off in the distance. And it is certainly not possible to grab hold of the fact that the six-lane road that bisects it was once an Indian trail. Oh, change would come, all right: it became a supply route in the War of 1812. Montrose was never to be left alone again. Two stagecoach runs met there. Now we ride the Tilt-A-Whirl, gravity sticks us to the sides as things go faster and faster, and then the bottom falls clean away.

IT'S THE DEBITAGE. The flakes of rock that are left after tools have been chipped from it. The obsolete, unimportant, forgotten, with moist green creeping across the surface of ever more new cracks that look old. The things that archaeologists gently brush the dirt from are the things that explain, if we can get past the amazement, the turnings on the path from then to now. And it could only be what remains of the past in a place—the residue of history covering many elements—that enables us to love it. Without the particularities that Time's March creates in a town (oh, Highland Square and Dodie's coffee shop; oh, art deco airport; don't ever leave me, little beach at Turkeyfoot Lake), there would be nothing to make it *itself* and thus nothing to pin your affections on. They slide right off the slick surface of the new.

Your home is what you see about you. It is composed only of things, which arrange themselves into visions. These visions then launch you into life, holding their banner so it streams back in the air to describe an arc from past through present. When the things get erased after you have already left the ground, you are no longer certain where you might land, because behind you is no trace of the spot whence you leaped.

Guard your hidden corners as gifts. You never know when they will be taken from your trembling hand. He parted the brambles grown over the path. *Down here, I have something to show you,* he said. Off the street in some backwater in the middle of town—not pejorative but true, as the gently shifting breeze blows from a few blocks away to your cheek the Little Cuyahoga's own molecules—we are walking into the past. My father is about to share with me his private treasure, something that still exists because no one cares if it does or does not. So we take it for our own. He shows me that the concrete bulwarks next to the path are not sewer walls, as I might think looking down at the moss-green water and its studding jewels of tires and old cans and a shopping cart and its flowing hair of ropes and weeds and plastic strips. No, this is the famous Ohio & Erie Canal, and there is what remains of Lock 15. And it is the reason for this particular wonderment: a building a century and a half old, which imagination alone knows to once have been white, now gray and asking with every splinter in its old clapboard to be allowed to sink to its knees and rest out eternity in the mud. The words "Meat Market" are just barely readable on the right of the facade. Ghosts are heavy in the air, because they love to congregate where they can blow your mind with improbabilities. This forgotten patch of overgrowth in a faded urban neighborhood there's no reason for others to go to was once the place everyone went to. Dozens and dozens of canal boats every day disgorged their passengers to tumble into the Mustill store—"Groceries & Provisions"—and buy what they could. What it was like to stand here and gaze upon this sight, knowing that for one hundred years of silence, few besides the raccoons and the vagrants ever did! But I knew even in that quivering moment that there were two ways it could go, because go it must. It had to vanish imminently in either way, and we had just happened on it when it still looked as though it could be ours forever. It was going to be torn down as a public hazard, or it was going to be saved. Much money would be expended on it, as Akron sought to do something with what evidence remained of her own birth. It would be "saved" with grants and carpentry, restoration and white paint, interpretive signage and landscaping, parking and new plumbing for the expectations of the modern visitor, brochures and an opening-day festival of bunting and speechifying. It would still be here, but it would be removed from our personal riches. At least I had it for one day.

Where are you to go now to feed the elemental hunger for solitude, for freedom from keeping your wheels in the slots provided for them, so you don't go anywhere (based on solid market research) that has not been decided for you? It feels like nowhere. There is deep despair among the loyal daughters of Akron. For one of them, there is even a roaring crowd in a stadium to hear. Alas, not anyone who has the power to do anything about it, even if their names should come somehow to light; and no one in the audience has ever been to Ohio. But look here at their response to the acid sarcasm in Chrissie Hynde's brass bell of a voice on the chorus, and you can see they have the wreck of their own private Akron in their hearts as they throw their fists into the air:

I went back to Ohio
But my city was gone
There was no train station
There was no downtown
South Howard had disappeared
All my favorite places
My city had been pulled down
Reduced to parking spaces
A, O, way to go, Ohio

Well, I went back to Ohio
But my family was gone
I stood on the back porch
There was nobody home
I was stunned and amazed
My childhood memories
Slowly swirled past
Like the wind through the trees
A, O, oh way to go, Ohio

I went back to Ohio
But my pretty countryside
Had been paved down the middle
By a government that had no pride
The farms of Ohio

Had been replaced by shopping malls
And Muzak filled the air
From Seneca to Cuyahoga Falls
Said, A, O, oh way to go, Ohio

THERE ARE SOME places left. Places they didn't get to, or couldn't, because they were in the godforsaken tangle of vines and saplings falling down the steep inclines carved by the prehistoric Little Cuyahoga. This was before it knew that the same eager hopeful who had plotted successfully a few years earlier to divert the Little Cuyahoga would again attempt to turn luck, and another of his millraces, into a place full of people and their money. He failed, because this millrace failed to race, and Summit City billowed to the earth like gossamer and was forgotten. It is today a park called the Chuckery, after a story that sounds too apocryphal to be true. (When a wag was asked the population of the new city, he reported, "A thousand: one man and 999 woodchucks.") But something happens to you when you go to the Chuckery. If you are alone there, and on any inclement weekday you will be, suddenly you realize something about your sight. It is no longer yours. Instead you see with the searching eyes of an aborigine, and this is a familiar landscape, like home. Nothing about it is frightening or needs to be tamed or made hospitable to your ventures: it is already everything you want. And as you stand in the footprints of this wraith, you realize nothing has changed here, by the banks of the swiftly moving river, for as long back as it is possible to grasp. This idea fills you. A quarter of a mile down the river is another time machine, a silent man with arms upraised and unmoving in order to give you the deep heebie-jeebies. He is just pretending to wear the garb of a white oak. They call him the signal tree. Well before the damnable concepts were hit upon that allowed our brazen thieves of forebears to make him silent, he gave voluble directions to anyone in moccasins who might be looking for the way to the high-water portage path a little bit east of the usual one between the Cuyahoga and the Tuscarawas.

We have retained our vernal tendencies to believe all endings are happy ever after. This has prevented us from seeing the rotting carcass of truth right in front of us: "progress" is just another word for larceny. ("All societies influenced by Western civilization are at present committed to the gospel of growth—the whirling dervish doctrine which teaches: produce more so that you can consume more so that you can produce still more. One need not be a sociologist to know that such a philosophy is insane," wrote René Dubos in 1968 in *So Human an Animal*, worth a Pulitzer but obviously no substantive action.)

Perhaps it is the persistence of beloved fairy tales, in which every child is discovered to be royal and will henceforth want for nought. Perhaps it comes from living in a country where for the first two centuries the plenty seemed without end. Whatever caused it, it now makes us look straight at the possibility of a real and imminent end to much of what we know (*the environmental study was written by 1,360 experts from 95 countries over the course of four years and reviewed by 850 authorities; still not convinced?*) and see nothing, absolutely nothing, new.

Once upon a time, endings were just beginnings seen from another place. There was a way to get around them to the other side. We recall our youth in the contented suburb as idyllic not because we stayed there but because we could leave. There were edges to it to look beyond, not so much toward anything but back into a collective past.

> In New England, for example, suburbs were built in clearings in the forest. Most of these forests grew on long-abandoned farms and were filled with old stone fences and the ruins of barns and wells. . . . In most of America, children could walk to the edge of the development and really find something else. This fact gave rise to one of the most common political phenomena of the age, in which

the most recent arrivals became most active in trying to stop further development, little realizing that their fellow citizens felt it was *their* houses that had ruined the town.

—THOMAS HINE, *Populuxe*

Well, I accept the name of hypocrite, but I keep on marching. I am like one of those raving lunatics who say such things as "America for Americans!" (who the heck are they referring to?) but whose grandparents came here on a boat. I am part of the problem, and I long for a solution. Every step into a future we have not chosen for ourselves but instead have had delivered to us as a hammer delivers a blow removes another experience from the list of possibles. The world used to belong to the people who lived in it. How strange! Seventy years ago people who had little money for anything but, say, their five boys and the purchase of the food they kept eating and shoes they kept wearing out still had weekend entertainments that to them felt as rich as anything you could order from the Sharper Image. They would motor out to the countryside, stop when they liked the view, and unfurl their old horse blanket in a farmer's field. No one would quickly pull up on an ATV and tell them it was private property. No yellow plastic posted signs issued every fifteen feet would have made them drive on. At least that is what my father told me about his family when he was young. They found solitude in the borrowing of what should never be owned.

Forty years ago, my mother could stop her car by the side of the road to gather Queen Anne's lace for a party bouquet, though she might have thought picnicking there would be a step too far. Thirty-five years ago a certain demented daughter would spend hours lost but found in the woods. It was lovely how many things could come to one's attention there. These days there are fewer and fewer places like "the woods," those generic spaces that didn't seem to belong to anyone but the kids and the squirrels. Instead it's one-acre lots demarked by stockade ("privacy") fence—no more the gentle punctuation of pickets, where needed; now it's a fort for the occupying army. You simply don't go there at all. Your mobility has been cut, and then cut again, until you're like the horse, whose native range is mile after mile but who now gets the same half acre of dusty paddock. Something bigger than you has caused this impoverishment, but all you can see are the sentry guards who have been posted to shoot anything that moves. And just try to get to the fragments of unowned place that still remain—whoosh! That was close; almost nailed by a car at 65 mph on the country byway. Each decade of the last century added another ten miles per hour to the accustomed speed, and another ten thousand vehicular missiles to the traffic, so that at this point you take your life in your hands to cross to your mailbox. Who in their right minds would let their children out to play all day unmonitored, so they might go wherever their sudden yearnings might lead?

At least they do get to go to their soccer game, even if it is bracketed by a car ride, like every single activity in their young lives. The other creatures whose happy wanderings have been done in by the apotheosis of the car have not been so lucky. Any scene painted before the early twentieth century will depict the common witness to all human life, the domestic canine, free to go where instinct and interest direct. It was hard to be run over by a speeding carriage, though a kick to the skull of any dog who worried a horse was a distinct possibility. It seems like a fair exchange. Now man's best friend spends a life in lonely frustration in the fenced backyard or, worse, in unspeakable misery unto psychosis, chained to the same twenty-foot patch of dirt. Dean Acheson in his memoirs decried what had been stolen after the time of his own youth, during the golden age of the first years of the last century: "the plunge into a motor age and city life swept away the freedom of children and dogs, put them both on leashes and made them the organized prisoners of an adult world." By the seventies, after the golden age of *my* youth, the robbery was complete.

Ah, the fifties. Surely it rivaled any storied empire's ripest heights. It is only coincidentally the time of my own growing up, so I may speak with authority. We were on the cusp of new worlds (I was on the cusp of solid food). Our televisions winked blue and white in the nighttime living rooms of our imaginations: the clatter of tiny hoofs across rocky desert, the lowing of longhorns, the whoops of redskins before they got the richly deserved minié ball in the chest to fall like rocks from the precipice, the buried message in every half-hour segment in this heyday of the potted Frontier West that we, too, were pioneers with only a few insensate obstacles to our possession of everything we saw to the horizon and beyond. The House of the Future opened at Disneyland in 1957, as I was mewling for my bottle.

How beautiful the box of Oxydol looks, how new and promising. You simply forget that you haven't seen this exact detergent in a while or that particular candy bar; you elide the years until it seems it was only moments ago. I sit with my son in my lap and read him a book. We reach the back cover and stare at it together, the list of other titles, the ring of animals and the elephant's red blanket . . . goodness. The duckie looks familiar. And that puppy! The camel, which I seem to have studied for years in some former life—I must have had one of these very books. I'm glad that my son is embarking on the same experience, absorbing every detail with his visual memory; I am glad that this still exists for him. Then I realize, Wait; I bought this in an *antiques* store.

The hunger to revisit the sensuous experiences of childhood—and the most potent are the most trivial, the things imbued with importance because we did not know they were unimportant—is increasing in proportion to the pace of our loss of them. Whole industries have come into being to satisfy it. My mother can't imagine why I feel such a mystical pull to the tartan-plaid enameled cooler I find in the pages of a catalog; she threw ours out in 1973 after too many years of loyal service. I suppose she could feel such desire only for some lost product of the thirties. But look at all this stuff (my breath catches) airlifted straight from

1959, bearing heavy tags and aimed squarely at the big buyers of my age. We want it all. Deep, satisfying purchases. Piece by piece we re-create the homescape of yore. This is what Restoration Hardware banks on. It sells precious little hardware, even less to restore anything with—but it restores home to us.

Right here in the story is the time to come to some beautifully articulated understanding that all of this is really a lot of folderol on top of a simple phenomenon that, approached head-on, would have telescoped the narrative shut as compactly as a travel drinking cup. It would predictably begin with etymology from the Oxford English Dictionary (*nostalgia*: from the Greek for "return home" and "pain"). It would find some poetic way to state an obviousness: isn't it strange how everyone's lamented Halcyon Days in the Homeplace just happened to coincide with the middle of their adolescence, the time when death was just a concept and life stretched on forever, no ruination in sight? Finally the point would be made that such longing for the lost world of one's shiftless youth boils down to nothing but the old fear of mortality. Yet somehow, it doesn't work to speak of the Ultimate Darkness in the same line as "when I was a kid a long time ago in Akron, Ohio." That seems almost tasteless, not to mention missing the gravitas that should accompany an epiphany. So we detour around this paragraph, excise it, and hope it doesn't leave a faint stain.

WE ARE A GENERATION weighed down by a sadness we do not know we feel. The promise was whispered melodiously in our ears sometime after the enjoyment of the great treasures beneath the TV dinner's foil and before the deep velvet of sleep in our soft, footed pajamas. The delivery, we have discovered by now, is not as we were pledged. The disparity is so geologic that we risk our necks in attempting to view the whole towering thing. The velocity of change has picked up a bit: no longer can we disregard it as some crumbling old history. What is lost was here just thirty or forty years ago, and thus it is written all over the page of your life. But still you don't know what can be done. Each announcement comes wrapped in its own fait accompli: this going, this coming, look out, look away, cry alone, it's done. The golf courses, the roads, the stores, the cutting, drilling, stripping. Your village in England sitting next to the planned town that grows ever upward, ever out. Your center city losing another century house and gaining one more superfluous drugstore behind its Indian Ocean of parking lot. Those old farms bearing new billboards of what's to come: forty huge houses of Frankensteinian architecture unmoored from any landscape to float just above its treelessness. Your ancient mountaintop a resort and vacation homes. That Beaux Arts post office a Popeyes Chicken and Biscuits. This revered battlefield fertilized with men's blood a shopping center. The dirt road paved. The paved road once two lane, now four; once four, now six. The crossroads with no light gets its signal. The march of time keeps marching, the army bigger every day.

The House of the Future was torn down ten years after it was built.

Garner's is a desiccated crumb of a memory, hidden under the seat cushions of an old sofa forgotten in the garage.

Our generation is the first in history to have witnessed a doubling of the world population in a single lifetime. It has never happened to anyone else but us, and it probably never will again. It is real, that choking breathlessness you feel, as if on an overcrowded elevator that is momentarily stuck. It is real, that childish despair on watching the things that made up a pleasant universe loaded onto a flatbed truck and getting smaller and smaller as it disappears down the highway, forever. It is real, the acceleration of loss.

Yes, there are places where the memories are settling in for the long term, flies in amber. The towns in the tall grasses of the prairie, where you can fairly hear the wind whistle down the empty main streets and the banging of the screen doors all morning against the frames of what were people's birth houses, now the crypts of what they remember. And some cities, too, whose numbers are actually declining. They have to paint lights onto the windows of buildings, lest the whole thing become a runaway car on the roller coaster of misfortune, taking everyone with it backward in time. Occasionally, the giving back to the earth of some small acreage here and there that had been used but not wholly ruined; perhaps the wildflowers and weeds, the crows and the fieldmice, just might call these few acres home again.

But in fact for every depopulated town, there are twenty counties losing their farmland and forest as fast as a broken main loses water. The figures stagger the brain, sort of like trying to conceive of the scope of our galaxy. For every place one might stumble on to discover the clocks have stopped in 1963 (Check it out! This dinner menu has cottage cheese as a side dish!), there are fifty more that have retained nothing older than three years ago. On a walk deep into the loneliest woods, the turn in the path now reveals not a sunny glade but Day-Glo surveyor's tape, and every tree of any girth bears a spraypainted bull's-eye. This is a metaphor. I also saw it today. What you know and love is finite. It is already slated for removal.

Deep down, my home, my cradle, is still where it always was. Your home is still within you, the box it made and then hid inside. I know nothing of its charms. I am too busy looking at the peculiar light of Akron. Suddenly it has an extravagance, a texture as it touches far walls of old factories, that does not exist anywhere else. Sitting on the back deck of the burger joint downtown, surrounded by a well of space and then the slanted sun hitting distant brick, I am in a haunt of familiarity, a place I have never seen. Here is what it comes down to: the pain of mortality and the ache of losing all we have come to know, both merged in the changing landscape of home. Now I know some kind of truth, but I cannot put it into words.

Ohio can absorb all amounts of sadness. That is what it is there for.

SINCE AN ACCOUNTING of home is an inventory of loss, start listing. Begin arbitrarily, say with your grandmother's house, a place of deep and gorgeous mystery. On the corner of Fir and Forge, it was once a fine address. It lodged five boys, saw the early death of their father, gave memories to forty cousins: of playing under the rose arbor, breaking the beds upstairs by jumping on them, the click of dominoes in the kitchen, taking naps on the sunporch after a wintergreen tablet "sleeping pill," nearly dropping dead of fear on catching sight of grandfather's great doctor's chart of the nervous system, the skinless round eyes burning anyone's who dared to look at this monster made of strings. All that's left of the house sits in an ashtray on a desk, a small glazed tile that one's sentimental father thought to pry from the fireplace surround. Behold the house's replacement, a symphony of Schelling's "frozen music" in yellow brick: Eshelman Legal Group, ground floor to let by Cummins Real Estate.

This sarcasm is the gesture of an extremist, as it is necessarily lost on everyone except the family circle, and they avert their gaze should they chance to drive down the old street. To all the rest there was never anything there but what is there now. It is possible that some, historically inclined, might emit a sigh upon coming across the small picture on p. 79 in *Akron: City at the Summit* (a production of the Summit County Historical Society), in which "Mr. and Mrs. Harvey S. Firestone and sons sat in a touring car on Fir Hill, circa 1908," but only if they noticed the squarely built stucco house in the background and realized that they can't place the location.

Spasms of uninteresting wailing on matters this small require their author to be told to get some perspective, or at least to put all the little losses inside the bag of the big, where they will be swallowed up. It is appropriate then to have spent childhood a short walk from what is known as the Treaty Line, which marks another of those specious "agreements" whereby some Indians had no choice but to stay to one side of a spot that was theirs from prehistory until one sudden day. The sign at the site reads: "In 1785 the Treaty of Fort McIntosh made this area a part of the United States. Portage Path became the boundary between the states and the Delaware and Wyandot Indians." "Made"; "became." I don't know, do these words contain the sound of crying to you?

A newspaper in 1817 opined that "the cessions made by the Indians on this occasion nearly extinguish their title to the state. . . . The two great objects gained; the security of the North Western frontier and an opportunity for an immediate settlement of the country which . . . will compel the few remaining Indians to adopt the habits of civilization, or to migrate to situations more congenial to savage life." Notwithstanding the fact that soon no such "situations" would exist anymore, and that it goes without saying that the treaty was immediately repudiated by most of the native people in Ohio. Nonetheless, the Wyandots attempted to conform to the fate offered them. They listened to the missionaries. The messages of Christianity contained a few familiar ideas. But there was no way to comprehend why the Creator, whose beloved offspring they were, would have written a book about strange lands and peoples in a language they could not read and then intended this book to dictate the abandonment of their lifeways after thousands of years. A Wyandot chief named Mononcue expressed his position by telling the whites, "I have some notion of giving up some of my Indian customs; but I cannot agree to quit painting my face. This would be wrong, and it would jeopardize my health."

Not even one who bemoans the onslaught of a condominium community or the expansion of the local ski area can quite grasp an idea like considering the land as the Great Self, which the Navajo did. The Creeks, cheated out of their homelands in Georgia and Alabama, determined to "die at the corners of their fences" rather than abandon the ground on which their forefathers had lived. Pushed to a small quarter of Alabama, they were described by a foreign visitor as "wandering about like bees whose hive has been destroyed." Many died after relocating.

The problem was theoretical as well as applied. As Toohul-hulsote of the Nez Perce observed, "You white people get together and measure the earth and then divide it." In the intervening century and a half, somehow someone figured out how to best Abraham Lincoln ("The land, the earth God gave to man for his home . . . should never be the possession of any man, corporation, [or] society . . . any more than the air or water"), and the most basic notions of the common good have vanished. Left completely out of the equation, since they more than anyone were not wise enough to get a controlling share of stock and then donate heavily to the election campaign, are the rest of the sentient beings who call this place home. Not that it matters much in the end. What would a bear or a mountain lion care about the freedom to write eloquent-but-futile letters to the local editor on the miseries of no longer being able to live as all of evolution prepared him to live? Has there been in recent memory a single subdivision stopped by even a river of tears?

You thought this might be a dark-tinged urban memoir about coming up from life in the gray ranch houses beside the railroad tracks of some hopeless trap of a dead industrial town that was tantamount to a grave for the brief bloom of youth? A far better story, I agree. Not much narrative arc to a tale of upper-middle-class happiness in a city, population 217,074, that lost its industry but moved quickly on to the "service professions" (sounding like the village where the folk took in one another's wash; at least everyone's got a job). I must apologize for the lack of some grit, some falling-down drunks in the family, something to cheer about (*a protagonist who doesn't whine!*). Our diversions were more genteel. That's "boring" to non-Akronites. But I assume you had yours, too. They make you sad to think about, don't they, and then redden your cheek in recognizing that?

I don't bewail the loss of any special ways of life; Ohio never had much that was specific to it. We didn't have a language, a mode of dress, a cache of recipes, a certain type of craft, or a personal mythology steamrolled by the same three monster corporations that have steamrolled everyplace else. We have been made bereft quite simply of *life*, the space and time and latitude to see and feel what was around. Oh, and also the "what" that was around: the vast green, the solace of knowing there were places that belonged primarily to some species other than man, the vestiges of history left in place, the hiding spots. There's no wandering anymore, because there's no place left to wander. Instead you get in your car and go to the same destination as 3,603 other people, and then you get back in your car and go back home. The kids are in your car with you, not walking back from school, and so have lost the chance to discover a shortcut through various backyards or develop a preference for walking on the ten inches of shiny old brick left between the curbstone and the tar in order to feel their feet on a piece of their hometown's industrial history. They don't have the long minutes passing each house during which to absorb the separate personality of each, the expression of windows and doors and wrought-iron balconies and certain sad pine trees by the garage. The houses in their new neighborhoods have blankness for personality, vinyl siding for depth. Somewhere in the ether it was decided it was preferred if no one felt anything anymore. Perhaps if our cars were made big enough we could be distracted by having to amass sufficient commodities to fill them and justify the useless space. If the environment is pulled up, chewed up, then extruded from the same tubes in the same factory, tacked up again where the original chance and evolution used to be, everyone will be much happier. So happy, in fact, they will not have noticed. They will not complain.

It has largely worked.

But how can we forget all that we were? Nature is man's

house, as that gray bungalow was your house, the first home that shaped every deep and significant thing about you. When that house is lost, vestiges of memory are bound to recur, trigger ineluctable sadness for the dead, then resubmerge. You'll never quite get through the mourning. Santayana says "home" is a concept of happiness.

"Dear little house that I have lived in, there is happiness you have seen, even before I was born. In you is my life, and all the people I have loved are a part of you, so to go out of you, and leave you, is to leave myself." Richard Llewellyn's *How Green Was My Valley* is not only the lean model on which were hung later, fleshy imitators of bestselling status, it is the novel form of the portent we have ignored at our peril. It's as if we were caught forever inside those movies that always end with a bang and a message. Of course! How could we *be* this stupid?

You are no longer certain if something happened to you long ago, or if your grandmother told you about something that happened to her long ago and it alchemized in the night in your impressionable head. So you visit her town. The two of you walk together as one, and suddenly there are more, and more, the echo of hundreds of footfalls along Furnace Street with each step you take. She is both gone and not gone, in you and beside you to frighten you with the presence of a ghost, your whole family trailing your progress in a line reaching back one hundred years. You hear the sound of keening, even if it is just the wind singing through the struts of the Y Bridge that hangs high over the valley of the Little Cuyahoga. There is no difference between your home and a lament.

One night you fly to another place. It just happens to be Detroit. You watch out the window as the pattern of lit-up squares below spreads to every corner, a flat plate of repeating lines. What else? What else is down there to have made this increase to such a vastness, each little light a family home, each family home a little light? Look in vain for an answer. Detroit is finally sufficient unto itself and speaks not to you. They live there because they have always lived there, because they were born there, and because to leave would be to have their hearts broken when they return. For they would find it gone, but there, and between the two a chasm that absorbs everything.

ADOPTED TOWN

His past came back to him in a flash and he remembered it all to the last detail. . . . It is hard to say what there was in that memory to produce so strong an impression on the poor general, who was, as usual, slightly drunk; but he was suddenly extraordinarily moved. "I remember—I remember everything!" he cried.

—DOSTOEVSKY, *The Idiot*

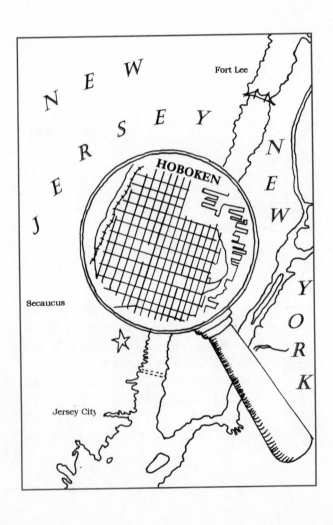

THE SMALL TOWN is situated between two tunnels to the big city. Cars direct themselves ever away, leaving only a memory of stirred air and black fumes. Then we are once more alone, furtive figures scuttling down back streets past old warehouses and pudding factories. An occasional light in one of them points to the infinitesimally small number of newcomers, the bad painters and plaster of paris sculptors who spend hours alone in their uncleaned spaces lit by bare bulbs. They are the vanguard of a new movement that will reshape this former island of swamp less than a mile across a big river from a glittering metropolis that has no idea whether it lives or it dies. But first they have to suffer.

This was in the beginning of the world, when everything was impossibly supple and emerald green. Our eyes, being new, transformed what was there into what we wanted. To a point.

One of these forlorn figures wore an oversized black herringbone man's coat with the cuffs turned back, which caused the lining to separate into a loose net of soft threads. It bore the label of a store in Cambridge, Massachusetts, evidence that its original owner, her father, had worn it at precisely this stage in his life, after the dam gates of school had opened and sent their yearly flow of students out toward the harbors of real life. We, too, went where the current took us, which in this case was literally down the Hudson about seventy-five miles, to stop where a knowledgeable and beloved and ever-so-cosmopolitan friend had said to stop. The newcomer would have followed this friend to the ends of the earth, so Hoboken did not really seem that bad. Besides, the friend had said over the wire stretching from her parents' house in New York all the way to the other's parents' house in Ohio, *I've looked everywhere, and we can't afford anything in the city, but lots of artists and musicians are moving to Hoboken—no, no, in New Jersey—and we can definitely find an apartment there.*

Yes, indeed, we could. Every single decade since 1910, the town had hemhorraged population. Two thousand, eight thousand, three thousand, nine thousand. It was like a skeleton still wearing its prom dress. Its housing hung slack over bones. The lovely brownstones of uptown were still intact, but we required something affordable, near the Port Authority Trans Hudson trains, and what was there was degraded. Thus we found ourselves at 122 Bloomfield Street, address of deep psychic ambivalence.

It was on the first floor, even though it exuded a distinct basementness. At first I lacked the vocabulary to properly term it a railroad apartment, and all I knew was that the interior rooms could have been used to safely process film. Light was what the polished brass starburst chandelier was for, the ultimate in early seventies hardware-store chic. Alas, the acoustical-tile ceiling had been dropped so far that some of our taller guests received cricks in their necks for party favors, and it made the light fixture a special hazard to anyone who neglected to turn it on before routing themselves through the room. Rarely was food prepared in what was determined to be the "kitchen," a crawl space wedged between one interior room and the back bedroom and set off by an accordion-fold door made of something like pressed paper that was secured with a magnet. Just as well, because the room really belonged to the vermin. We had a fine coffeepot, however.

The dear friend had inexplicably chosen for her bedroom the front room, a couple of feet from the curbstone and separated from it by only the filmiest of materials. The building marked itself as among the city's finer by having actual heat, albeit stuck on the fry setting. This magnified the feeling that we were living in underground rooms near the location of some mighty boiler. Since she had opted to sleep on the sidewalk, this left me the large, light-filled, wood-floored back bedroom. It comprised a more recent if inscrutable addition to the building, and it suited the apartment about as well as new fingernail polish on a dead body. But it accommodated a white-painted hollow-core door on sawhorses for a magnificently sized desk, while fruit crates (no innovator I) held the books I had collected in philosophy and art-history courses and would no doubt never look at again. I very hopefully purchased a double bed. My half of the rent was $187.50.

Twenty-four years have passed since I first dragged my suit-case and boxes through a low doorway and onto the undulating green linoleum of my first apartment in a foreign land. I am sad to report there were several more to come. It is thirteen years since I managed to escape my second home, not really all that long ago, but to me the duration feels unspeakably ancient, like I closed up a trunk in another life, so I don't know what I'll find when I open it again. Maybe my lost youth will rise up and point a trembling finger at me and shriek in unearthly tones: You! You strangled me in Hoboken and left me there to die!

Only I could have made my most promising years the dark-est, the time of great beginnings the nadir of my existence. I had unwittingly chosen the one square mile of continental United States that could so perfectly mimic an inner landscape of despair that the two of us merged into one lonely, unpeopled, gray expanse of decrepit lostness.

The place you live is the era you live there, for how to separate the two? Thus Hoboken *is* the nineteen-eighties. And the place you live is also the age at which you live there. So it is the eighties in my twenties. Every goddamn rat hole, each asbestos tile on every blank tenement front, all those lonely pieces of trash blown against the broken fence of an abandoned park by an unheeding November wind: me, in the prime of life, in a place that became my portrait.

We LIVE IN a town that is the misused back alley of some other, better place. Our town is the place you pass through, averting your gaze. It is the place they forgot to clean, forgot to love, forgot. At its edges you will always find a lonesome gas station that will sell you gas of uncertain quality if only you would stop, always warehouses that look abandoned but that still emanate unplaceable smells, always the bump of derelict trolley tracks. An empty road rises up the hill toward Jersey City, where it becomes the eerie remnant of a long-ago age: the Paterson Plank Road. Imagining a time when the clatter of hoofs and wagon wheels were heard here against the planks of a wooden highway laid over the muck of a fertile land shakes you deeply.

Long rows of unadorned brick or wood-frame tenements march down the streets all the way to the vanishing point. Some had been "fixed up" with tarpaper siding that now falls off in strips, or an inferior product in wide use over all the land that is advertised as Garden State Brickface, or equally depressing, ersatz, and thin wrought-iron railing. There are no trees, as telephone poles are deemed to suffice. Their webs of sagging black wires cast thin shade on broken sidewalks that make a stroll a trek across blinding desert sands. Each neighborhood has its own weather.

Back on Adams Street it is always August, the bearing down of heat unrelieved by any shade almost impossible to take; the air is a sulfurous yellow. Uptown on Washington Street, meanwhile, it is hard winter as you pass the one beautiful building in town, the Episcopal church, beautiful because with its green lawn and gothic iron fence and lovely dark facade it suggests somewhere else far away. Coming upon this block reminds you of how far you have yet to walk in the weighty polar air. But around the desolate Church Square Park in the middle of town, which is not the middle of anything but rather the center of an absence, it is forever late fall after a rain, possessed of an ugly chill that gets into your bones and from there your soul. In that way it cements the sight of blown leaves and wrappers and bare trees and dog-stained dirt to the feeling that you are so unhappy you'd like to die.

This is the place from which I could find no egress for eleven long years. This is the place I would gladly return to so I could be young again and ever hopeful that one day soon I was going to bust out of there with my wings spread, to go high above the Hudson and wave to the Statue of Liberty on my farewell circuit of the places I'd been, now made more lovely by distance and the shimmering of the air.

How short a time, really, since this little place was missing its own golden youth. It certainly was beautiful then, though it took some canny blandishments to make others see it so at first. Hopoghan Hackingh was to the natives the "place of the tobacco pipe," but to Michael Pauw, the burgomaster of Amsterdam in 1624, it was another place to buy, no matter that it was not for sale. One hundred and twenty-five years later, after a somewhat bitter exchange of overseers, the royal governor, Jonathan Belcher, sized up eastern New Jersey: "Take the province in the Lump, it is the best country I have seen for men of middling fortunes, and for people who have to live by the sweat of their brows." And so it remained to my day—both a Lump and attractive solely to the man of middling fortune. See, another two hundred and thirty years and we are a motley bunch of strays, a few who will manage to start successful careers in the creative arts, the remainder crippled by emotional maladies that are not entirely apparent on the outside, just proved by the length of time we remain mired in the same spot.

In 1784 the estates of the Bayard family, King's Loyalists, were auctioned to the highest bidder. Thus, as a spoil of war, they came into the possession of one Colonel John Stevens. Upon the high bluff of Castle Point he built his delirious castle, then set about making even more money. First he commandeered the important ferry line to New York. Then in 1804 he sought to capitalize on Manhattan's fears of yellow fever and went to the dark streets of the city to shill plots in healthy Hoboken.

In the Elysian Fields, he gave people something to resort to. Such bucolic tranquillity! Along River Walk the ladies and gents, recently poured from the ferry's gangway, strolled up and back. They would sit on the shady grounds of the Colonnade Hotel and drink milk fresh from its own herd of Jersey cows. They would repair to Sybil's Cave, a freshwater spring (a drinkable spring! in Hoboken!) mined and turned into a tourist draw by the colonel, for a cup of purity at a penny apiece. Trees, which after all are lovelier than poems, held power over the scene. In a little book by Dr. Rudolph Rabe called *The Hoboken of My Boyhood*—how the title creaks with already aged and sadly musty nostalgia—the time of its glory is described. The New York Yacht Club had its clubhouse by the river. Beyond Eleventh Street were not factories and warehouses, highways and cracked streets, but the font of paradise, "proud in the majestic presence of magnificent oak trees, tulip, sycamores, and others." Many claim the first game of baseball was played here, but it was deemed of little matter to the people who in 1938 put a coffee-roasting plant on top of the site, or to their early-twenty-first-century offspring who plan to install the current Holy Trinity—condos, chain stores, and parking spaces—on the site of the former factory. (Says adspeak, "the last remaining significant parcel of developable space on New Jersey's Gold Coast.") Christopher Morley's *Seacoast of Bohemia,* a 1929 rendition of this earlier fabulous time, describes the "first resort" of New Yorkers—via ferry, "in five minutes you are in the country." And proving that developers will always have the last laugh on wise men, sages, and well-known writers, his opinion that "'quaint,' thank God, is the last thing Hoboken will ever be" is lent humorous irony by the changes wrought on the town within fifteen years of my own landing on the coast of a last true bohemia. For better and worse, believe me.

But first Hoboken had to be destroyed, at least before it could be destroyed again. By the time of the Civil War, the ogre of commercial "progress" was on its own stroll, and it cannot abide a beautiful scene being left to those who might possibly enjoy it. The trees must go. Boathouses too. The shad fishermen's shanties, a distant picture of elemental timelessness, made futureless. Sybil's Cave boarded up and soon to be forgotten but still there somewhere under the pavement trod by the uncaring; would that they had souls so they could be properly haunted. Transatlantic shipping was going to give Hoboken its new future, and when, a hundred years on, the advent of containerized shipping rendered useless its short piers, it was too late to return to Elysium. Adam and Eve had to get dressed.

Look to the south: Bayonne, too, used to be a green and breezy resort of city dwellers. Bayonne, yes, Bayonne! Crowd upon crowd of oil refineries and chemical factories—who invited you? Looking at the scene today and trying to superimpose the image of what had been, an effort that breaks most brains, may cause wonderment at a truly amazing thing: New Jersey's unique ability to pulverize itself into unrecognizability, to buy and sell its own body until it is a used-up, syphilitic junkie, an American Untouchable. It takes *work* to do such a job that not even a fragment is left of what used to be, by so many accounts, a transporting beauty.

Still, we must not oversimplify (even if New Jersey invites

it, by gum!). In its earliest conception, Hoboken was a place mainly to get into and then out of again. It was a ferry terminus, a railroad station, a shipping port, the end of the trolley lines. It is marked by the half-buried remains of tracks, tracks, tracks. It was the funnel through which poured three million soldiers aimed at the lines of World War I Europe. "Heaven, Hell, or Hoboken," they chanted, aptly situating the town near Purgatory. Around the turn of the previous century, Gustav Kobbé observed, in *Jersey Central*, "It may be said that thousands of the best citizens of New York are not citizens of that city at all; in the evening they ebb away." And toward what? "Hoboken, New Jersey, across the Hudson River from New York City, might be geographically termed a suburb, but it boasts few more suburban amenities than the Bowery in New York," opined *Fortune* in 1953.

But of course the land has been obliterated. Hoboken was once, at least at high tide, an island formed by marsh and creek at its western side. Nothing of that was left to remain except, perhaps, the mosquitoes.

Into and out of it transited the waves of foreigners: German, then Italian, then Puerto Rican, then white and young and "upwardly mobile." None liked the other. The problem was that those who should have been displaced neglected to leave. Epithets and sometimes harder things were thrown. Hoboken's "renaissance" was set to begin, only we did not know it.

WE ARE THE Island of Misfits. We are members of a peculiar club who recognize, warily, one another. We observe the customs of the town, which over time became entrenched as tradition, then law: it is here and here only that stop signs *become completely invisible*. Once entering the precincts of the Mile Square City, one is forbidden from even pretending to see them. This way, it is possible to achieve utmost velocity up Garden Street from First to Twelfth without having to pause at every other block. One is only

forced to screech to a stop before entering the tunnel-bound traf-
fic on Fourteenth Street due to a moderate risk of collision with a
Red Apple bus to New York (twenty-five cents cheaper than NJ
Transit, I am excited to learn).

We know the rule of getting groceries at the Shop Rite on the
corner of Washington and Newark as if by instinct: inspect bag of
cookies carefully for telltale ragged holes caused by diminutive
but sharp cutting teeth and crumbs issuing from same. Perhaps a
tiny German oompah band had accompanied the previous night's
gay revelry at the rodent feast. Because this is Hoboken in the
eighties in my twenties, it goes without saying that I stand in line
to pay with a trembling in my limbs and downcast eyes, lest they
meet the gaze of another one of us, the desperate prowlers for
human companionship and ecstatically biological union. It is
what I want more than anything in the world, except for recognition and fame, so that is why I avert my look.

Yet we do well to caveat emptor, at least a bit: most of us have
been tossed off the isle of Manhattan as defective, and it is DNA-
wise never a good idea for one muck-up to mate with another. We
are the type of people who long to be writers or musicians or
actors but who have trouble landing or keeping, much less
advancing from, jobs as menial workers. We end up serving bur-
rito specials to one another. Mistakes are almost made: the
apparently good-looking guy on the top floor who invites you over
for dinner in his cozy lair reveals that he *is* an actor, though he
seems to spend most of his time in a tux on the ground floor of
Macy's assaulting hapless customers with cologne. Somehow,
over the next weeks and months, he loses his looks bit by bit, as
well as his talent, until he is a loser par excellence, the sight of
whom down First Street causes you to quickly alter course up Willow to Second and then back down to First on Clinton, and hope
he hasn't gathered his junk mail from the box with the broken top
and stopped to chat up some other Hoboken neophyte who is
desirous of forthcoming friendship. The memory of his initially
cozy apartment, too, becomes over time the kind of suffocating

straitjacket you wake in dreams from only to find your comforter over your face and sweat slicking your hair. The weirdo crank is just another Hoboken tradition: an oddball by the name of Hetty Green lived on Washington Street in a mean cold-water flat; she died in 1916 with a hundred million to her name.

Does it say something about the human mind under duress that so many of your desired cohorts were held in such esteem by you they were virtually unapproachable? Remember, we are talking about young people who lived in tenements *in Hoboken*, not the better, more desirable, decrepit tenements of young people across the water. But the longer you stayed in this small pond, the bigger some of the fish appeared. All of them swam around in a place called Maxwell's.

Depending on the wind and the barometric pressure, the scent of burned coffee hung in the air even way back near the projects in the most forgotten quarter of the town, a mile and a half from the Brobdingnagian neon cup spilling its last drop of Maxwell House coffee on the waterfront by Sinatra Drive. But on the Eleventh Street side of the club, which our literary bible *The New Yorker* patted itself on the back for cleverness in calling "the best club in New York," the odor of coffee was replaced by something more . . . *immediate* coming from the dumpsters that held the progressively more inedible matter from the restaurant inside. Never mind. There were potent ways of dispelling the smell as you stood about on the street between sets or hoped to catch a glimpse of a certain someone who might or might not be coming tonight, he wasn't sure and sure wasn't going to tell you.

Inside, the jukebox was thrumming. It marked the formal beginning of the line waiting to pay for entry into the small, dark back room—or wait, is this the line to the women's toilet? because that was often longer, there being only one, and this a nightclub after all. There, on vinyl 45s, were all your faves: Hank Williams Sr., the Clash, the Beach Boys. Dropping a quarter in allowed you to demonstrate your rarefied aesthetic to the gathered crowd. Hanging on the exposed brick (should that be Exposed Brick™?)

above the machine was an unspeakably beautiful painting of New Jersey's epic landscape, the sky smeared pink and mauve above the smelters and gray shapes of manufacturing necessity.

Your watchful vigil was suspended once inside the back room, where it was too dark to see who was there, although over time you actually developed a sixth sense: the ability to detect, through what seemed, impossibly enough, *eyes in your skin,* his entrance into the closeness of the room. You knew he was there, somewhere behind you, buoyed up by the crowd, and this lent a poignant energy to your compulsive bouncing to the backbeat. There was no way to stop it, since the music was so fine, so perfect, so knowing and brilliant and transportingly exciting in its intelligence, that it was causing your thoughts to rise up in pointy shards like those of icebergs the size of continents crashing in polar waters. You knew you were witnessing the heights that art was wont to reach, and you *understood* it, every microscopically thin layer of intention sitting on another. One small voice among the many that spoke simultaneously—all perfectly well heard—in your brain was saying, "You might be the only person in the world who understands this so beautifully that your head is actually being hurt by the pinging of the molecules loosed by this creative act of comprehension!" Or something to that effect.

Indeed, it was a good time to be around and in your twenties and in the back room of Maxwell's. Sonic Youth. Beat Rodeo. Certain General. REM. The Replacements. Mission of Burma. An underground railroad from the Hoboken of the midwest, Cleveland, and the Hoboken of the south, Athens, gave tickets to the young people who would come to the real Hoboken and re-form into musical consortiums of overspilling talent: Antietam; the Feelies; the Bongos; the dBs; Human Switchboard. You were in Maxwell's so often to the accompaniment of the era's best bands it was like Mozart having come to play a little something in your living room. And because music could not contain all that there was to be said and experienced and processed about life's unbearable ironies, there were other things to be seen in the back room of Maxwell's. A young artist—her name turned out to be Nan Goldin—presented a work in progress she was calling "The Ballad of Sexual Dependency," a slide show of color pictures of her friends and their intense doings with one another and solitariness in the midst of others (this you understood all too well, although in the pictures it carried a glamour lacking completely in your own loneliness), paced to a musical sound track and representing a new kind of *gesamtkunstwerk* that made you almost breathless with realization. A showing of Tarkovsky's *Solaris*, the visual lusciousness of which made you write something about wanting to lick the screen. You would always go home and scribble in the film notebook you had started because you, you alone, had so much to say about the movies you were consuming like necessary meals. Here the film projector was a presence in the room, ticking and spinning, as you sat rapt on a metal folding chair.

On the nights you did not go there, of course, you went to the PATH station. One half block to the corner of Bloomfield and First, turn left and go past the looming brown City Hall, cross Washington Street and take in Shop Rite with your peripheral vision, then walk the half block between the main drag and Court Street—a mews of stables and carriage houses that extended half the length of the city and which was the one place in Hoboken you really wanted to live. This put you in front of the record store called Pier Platters. Some stores could be as intimidating as those churches of alien religions with rituals to which you were not privy, leaving you bound to violate them immediately just by opening the door. Such was Pier Platters to you, because you did not know how deep the waters of the musical ocean were. You feared falling off the end of the dock and realizing you could not swim, with your thin knowledge of a few bands that happened to play the couple of places you frequented. You might find yourself thumbing through a bin of used EPs aware you had never heard of a single one of these many performers. To reject them all would be to broadcast your ineptitude. To select a single unknown might expose you to the scathing silence of the clerk who just saw you pick the one total dog in the whole place. Not to mention having to take it home and listen once to something that would punish you well for wasting three very precious dollars.

As you started down the steps into the PATH station, a whooshing sound might announce you were about to see the lights of the Manhattan-bound train disappearing into the tunnel. You had yet to fit your dollar bill into the slot that usually spat it back, and you had yet to run down another flight of stairs without tripping. This could cost you fifteen minutes of waiting time, and when you had all the time in the world, giving away fifteen minutes of it was altogether too much to bear. (Now, in your dotage, with your remaining moments numbered, you can wait and wait again.) But it was far, far worse on the other end of things. Then it would be the dregs of the evening and near three in the morning, with the trains not even half as frequent, and the stations just made for torture. Ninth Street was the one at which you most often found yourself, all the worthwhile places in the world being below Fourteenth Street on this island that represented the promised land you would never attain. It was here that your formulation of atheism first began taking shape. For nothing you had ever done to any living creature would have brought forth this level of retribution from any just god. The entrance was a long sloping tube through which you were pulled, hair suddenly airborne and seeking to leave your head, by the sucking wind that gathered strength as your train departed forever. There was the lingering smell of today's lamb being slow roasted with oregano and garlic, courtesy of the kitchen vent from Balducci's fine groceries, located on the street just above. Quickly you learned not to bother running madly down the passageway at the sound of a train entering the station. It was crushing to have expended that energy and risked your ankles in your cowboy boots or vintage d'orsay pumps only to get that much closer to a train that was still going to leave you pushing against the turnstile that won't give because the change machine has rejected your dollar bill yet again. If it was prior to eleven, you might find yourself thinking you were lucky—

you made the train!—coming within inches of leaping aboard, before seeing that the lighted letters above the door indicated it was bound instead for Jersey City. In any event, there was a long wait ahead. The benches were already taken on one side by someone sleeping off a drunk and on the other by one homeless person with three large bags or by four sad and tired women who had just gotten off their jobs as office cleaners. So you walked down the platform to lean against one of the steel beams that acted as a column and tried not to fall asleep or cry. One of the people you had recently met was a talented but typically Hoboken-strange cartoonist who immortalized this awful evening rite by picturing a person very much like yourself waiting in the PATH station, cobwebs stretching from head to column.

In the early years, this did not have the same soul-deadening capacities it would come to have, like the place in the movie of your life where it becomes apparent that the main character is someone for whom not even the simplest thing can go right and who is destined to ride a trajectory heading always down. In the early years this did not matter so much because you still had your glorious friendship. You wore your mother's thin-waisted dresses from 1956 and sometimes ribbons in your hair. Everyone you met was just starting out, too. You still had everything.

WE LIVED IN Hudson County, the most densely settled area of a state that is the most densely populated in the nation. It is a place that doesn't want to let you go. Its streets take you one direction and then another and finally down this way, bleaker and bleaker and bleaker, until you are lost in the oldness and sadness the same way you would be lost if you fell into the featureless pits of a dead strip mine. You were only trying to get somewhere else. But here you are in Eliot's "Unreal City / Under the brown fog of a winter dawn," or is it Union City, where you had taken a wrong turn attempting to traverse Weehawken and eventually get to the bridge so you could go over the water and get to another state where the signs made sense and did not try deliberately to send you to a hell of brick buildings and underpasses and roads that split four ways, none of them the one you need to go. These towns all had the look of something that had died some time ago, a carcass baking under hot sun, left for the buzzards to pick clean. And indeed they would: the county politicians could be found chattering and hopping about, each taking their mouthful of graft and corruption. The smell of it all kept everyone away.

The people who lived in the precincts of Hudson County could not be made to care much.

> Crisscrossed by railroads and elevated highways, it has the appearance of a place to pass through rather than live in. . . . The drabness, dirt, and smell of the town are at first overpowering. . . . The lack of character is apparent from a glance when the consensus of elements thought distinctive by Jersey City people is compared with the same diagram for Boston. The Jersey City map is almost bare. . . . Again and again, subjects repeated that "nothing special" came to mind, that the city was hard to symbolize, that it had no distinctive sections. . . . *Much of the characteristic feeling for Jersey City seemed to be that it was a place on the edge of something else.*

Perhaps that last sentence doesn't need my emphasis, but I gave it anyway, because it is the only line of poetry ever written that fully explains this piece of eroded place: *on the edge of something else.* In the late fifties some researchers finally went around and asked people the most important thing of all: what the places they lived in felt like. Of the three cities studied, Boston, Los Angeles, and Hoboken's twin, Jersey City, the latter was found to be peculiarly poorly differentiated or "imageable," as the study has it. Its denizens' recall of its layout was far worse than those in the other two cities: "Many descriptions of the scene by established residents, young or old, were accompanied by the ghosts of what used to be there. Changes, such as those wrought by the freeway system, have left scars on the mental image."

But of course: New Jersey sold its soul to the devil for as many cars as it could drive. Even if you move far, far away, the sight of a bile-yellow license plate will call up a particular apprehensiveness, a yucky feeling in the gut, and not only to do with the justifiable fear that this car is going to try to rear-end you. It is almost as if you could see a communicable disease: *oh, my god, here comes New Jersey!* Whatever they have is about to infect you, and then your place will look like theirs: nothing but concrete, houses, driveways, garages, apartment buildings, roadways (10,700 miles and counting!) lined with strip malls as far as the eye can see, highways, glass office blocks, and the occasional tree they haven't cut down yet. Fifty thousand acres of open space go under the bulldozer every year, and there certainly can't be much left at that rate. It is known as "The Garden State."

In the early nineteen-twenties Edmund Wilson proved it was impossible to have too low an estimation of New Jersey. Just a few of his compliments: "an atmosphere of tarnishment and mess"; "indifferent and dingy"; "the door-mat, the servant, and the picnic-ground of the social organisms which drain it." He could have been standing on Washington Street in Hoboken, or indeed on the brink of many vistas in the state, when he noted "it is characteristic of New Jersey that not even the horrible here attains really heroic proportions." A later but no less great New Jersey writer, Luc Sante, rephrased this appreciation with the apposite term "militant blandness."

My aim, obviously, is not to pick on New Jersey. It is just that this one state alone has crystallized, brought to a breathtaking new level, the attempts of the entire country to look the other way while anything that was here at the Dawn of Time finally gets the heave-ho in favor of something people can turn into money. It has taken on the flavor of an addiction: we just can't help ourselves. One sixth of all Americans derive their livelihood from cars, whether making them, selling them, equipping them, filling them, fixing them, or disposing of them.

Finally we fall backward, heads dully throbbing, with figures and incomprehensible trivia drooling down our chins: *America has paved 3.9 million miles of road, equivalent to 157 times around the equator; every 5 new cars we make, a football-field-size bit of land gets covered with asphalt; 3 million, yes million, acres of open space are developed each year in this country; farmland is lost at the rate of 2 acres per minute; someone just entering middle age now who grew up in, say, Rockland County in New York lived in a place with 17,360 acres of farmland—now there are 250, but check back in a few minutes.* We can only compile the statistics and get out of the way, dumbfounded. No one knows what to do about it. There is nothing to do about it. The newspapers fill with stories containing incredible facts; apparently no one reads them. Occasionally there is an account of some monumental fight actually won, costing years of sweaty effort, and the prize is one development scaled back, one farm saved, a few acres that won't be logged, a Civil War battlefield protected though with givebacks, a single Wal-Mart backburnered. Meanwhile, scores of houses, health clubs, hospitals, and convenience stores and 2,378 Wal-Marts went up elsewhere. Lewis Mumford a long time ago seemed amazed that we were doing what we were doing, as if he believed that we could control ourselves: "We have consistently acted as if there were no relation between the number of people we dump on the land and the amount of congestion on the streets and arterial traffic routes." Be indignant all you want at the insensible idiocy of every one of us, but to stop our headlong slide into self-destruction only two things need be done: stop people from procreating with such abandon, and change our form of governance and its supporting economy. (Simple!)

The big numbers only fit through the brain edgewise and so cannot in fact be processed. We are made for smaller stuff: what we see in the several yards around us, what it makes us feel. The emotional space to catch one's breath, the vacant apartment that might be lent to someone who will do something artistically big in it, the quietly forgotten corners of town that are not overnight sold and flipped half a dozen times in the weeks before transformation into the next hot neighborhood for the rich—there is only a sense that these things are gone never to return, but our sadness does not look for the reason. What is it but a stare at the galaxies above, unable in any real way to comprehend their distance, to know that the planet is about to add three *billion* more people? Not much easier to try to think of what this country alone will be like with 120 million more people, even if you imagine all of them competing for your parking space at the post office. We won't speak of the fact that you will never again be able to visit the lovely beach of your childhood, because you can't get near it. (And no, no simpler to think of the two million more scurrying humans soon to be paving over their own little piece of Great Britain, either; or the three to eight million added to Australia; nor, certainly, the 300 million destined for India.) Perhaps the only thing that can be grasped by any one of us is the sight of bulldozers just down the lane, grading the former hay meadow and giving rise to a dream vision of thirty-seven new taupe vinyl-sided "homes" with white trim and yawning bays for several cars. Then we might begin to see the future. It is composed of permanent mourning and unhappy accommodation.

THERE WAS ONE WAY to have known this was coming. It was buried in the local news and letters-to-the-editor sections, which you should have been reading instead of believing the world news was somehow more important. Nothing has more impact on life than the fate of the neighbor's hydrangea. When the whingeing (known by psychologists as projection) grows to a fatal pitch that it's every other species of animal that has overpopulated and now must be put to death, we can be confident that our overrunning numbers have finally exceeded pestilential levels.

Something gets into you, and you want to yank on the collars of people in the street until their eyeballs make noise. You mean to horrify them with the news, amply documented if they cared, that the earth is pretty much a goner. What you do instead is convince them of your lunacy.

And surely they would have a point. You have been filling file folders labeled "Death to the Earth!" for a little too long. It's damaged you; perhaps it's an addiction, because you feel a weird happiness every time you can get your scissors around another one. GLOBAL WARMING THREATENS TO KILL OFF A MILLION SPECIES: SCIENTISTS EXPRESS SHOCK AT SCALE OF DISASTER. (Long ago you discovered that *The Guardian Weekly* is the only paper that can satisfy this jones, possibly because it does not derive a huge income from selling Cadillac Escalades and eight-bedroom "homes" like some other papers that mysteriously remain respected, and so your files are stuffed with its thin newsprint.) You pull out a magazine ad—fashionably half-clad, thin, and bronzed young people draped about a rain forest, bearing the legend "Nature: Love it while it lasts"—and something funny starts happening in your head. You think it's not what the good people of Diesel had intended.

Suddenly now it hits, bizarrely easy to grasp. *We are inexorably headed for the Big Goodbye.* It's official! The unthinkable is ready to be thought. It is finally in sight, after all of human history behind us. In the pit of what is left of your miserable soul you feel it coming, the definitive loss of home, bigger than the cause of one person's tears. Yours and mine, the private sob, will be joined by a mass crying; whole cultures, ways of life, languages, beliefs, landscapes, climates, now falling at a cataclysmic rate along with millions of trees in the Congo basin and the Brazilian rain forest and along the Mongolian border. The echo of their crashing is a prelude to the final kiss-off, the extinction of our species along with every other that is made to suffer by us. Perhaps we have simply spent too long with our feet on the pedals of those aggressively propulsive machines that we have come to think there is no thing, no creature, we can't blast right through, over, or past, while remaining immune to the air we have stirred or the sorrow we have caused. In fact, we have become so numerous at last that our native inability to stop our rapacious grasping of anything we want—the earth as discount store—is tipping the balance. The planet's miraculous powers of regeneration are the magician's trick unveiled and rendered useless: in just fifty years we have managed to degrade at unprecedented velocity the physical attributes of the only place we have. Sixty percent of our natural resources are in danger; almost a third of animal species are on the way out. Gone. All the birthplaces will be changed and thus gone. The weeping will form a deluge. Then quiet.

DRIVING ALONG ITS roads—since there is a good chance that that is all you would be doing in the state—it comes to mind: How did New Jersey get to be New Jersey? This is a little like asking how did Renoir get to be Renoir. If New Jersey's exquisitely practiced art is to mold itself to the lowest common denominator, then to understand it you must go back in time to study the art's history. To start with now would be to induce gibbering in the unprepared: b-but how could this happen? How did we become a nation that universally aspires to a suburban château in a sidewalkless gated "community," nothing less than ten thousand square feet will do, and at that size needs two laundry rooms not to mention a five-car garage? (HOUSEHOLD SPRAWL POSES THREAT, STUDY SAYS: "The number of people in the average household is shrinking, driving an international housing boom that puts more strain on biodiversity and the environment than does the overall rise in the world's population, according to a study recently published in the journal *Nature*.") Since 1970 average American families have shrunk by 15 percent while their houses have grown 50 percent bigger. But what looks suspiciously like simple greed, in cahoots with sheer tastelessness, is actually more complicated.

First, you have to knock people over the head to make them senseless. Then you give them drugs so they can't actually use their brains. Then you can sell them the idea of sprawl! And just about anything else! For instance, a Cadillac Escalade!

In the twenties we found ourselves moving from an industrial to a postindustrial economy, one based on ideas and services. Since at least the Great Depression, American business has been worrying that workers couldn't afford the goods they produced. What to do? Why, make them believe they *have* to have those things. Enter the science of advertising: in 1929, advertising was a $1 billion business; by 1962, it was $12 billion. But that's peanuts. Now the world spends $350 billion per year on this worthwhile endeavor; it even sells America its elected officials. It wouldn't be half as successful without a good delivery system, and more perfect ones than the television and computer would be hard to invent. They allow the efficient mainlining of that "Buy!" message by first rendering the viewer neurologically helpless to resist any blandishment, no matter how idiotic or damaging to himself or the planet at large. Better yet, all three—it's today's trifecta.

Pretty perfect, too, for a species that naturally does not care for consequences and that doesn't like to locate causes—not in ourselves, anyway. (Psychotherapy is quaint or else deserving of ridicule; learning from history is beyond the capabilities of a people who desire only more time with their Game Boys.) If we don't have to look at it, it isn't there. Trash vanishes from our cans in the middle of the night, never to be seen again. Reports on TV state facts—"The ozone layer is apparently disappearing at a much faster rate than previously believed! More after these messages"— as if they were the weather or a traffic jam out on highway 57. We have yet to experience the full extent of what we, along with our toys, have wrought. Like the ideal cartoon character, our legs will keep churning through midair, and we will fall only after we see the abyss open beneath our feet. "As we're enjoying consumer society, most of us don't think about the negative consequences of having too much enjoyment in life," understates a Yale psychiatry professor in an article on global warming in *The New York Times*, in which the reporter digests the findings of researchers who believe "the ethos of American life, hammered into people's heads by credit card companies, carmakers and fast-food sellers, is to buy now, consume now, live now, and whatever you do don't put off the gratification."

All too rarely is there a satisfying ending put to the tale, the kind that Hollywood always assures. Almost never do our actions turn around and immediately bite us in the ass, as they should. One exception is Lyme disease–carrying ticks, their increase due to the fragmentation of woodlands by house building. They have been known to aim appropriately. So, too, with lethal jellyfish, whose populations have lately been booming. It's not nice to mess with Mother Nature.

But this is too little, too late. We have already contravened every law of nature, including the supreme proscription. We have taken to befouling our own nest. What kind of creature would do that?

The short answer is, one that would countenance the existence of something like Wal-Mart. The world's largest retailer; the world's largest private employer; the world's largest corporation. More than 60 percent of everything that is bought here is bought there. Of course, the figure might be larger were it not such an execrable experience to shop in one, with the glaring lights over linoleum and painful explosions of sound over the PA system asking for help in the toaster aisle and sad worn-down clerks moving endless miles of cheap goods as if in slow motion over the bar-code sensors that electronically transfer glee back to headquarters in Bentonville. In some kind of true achievement, the Supercenters can fill 220,000 square feet. In another, their masterminds have been planning to open one every other day. If zoning doesn't permit consumer cathedrals of that size, they fly them in under the radar in the form of the comfortingly named Neighborhood Market, a hypertrophied 7-Eleven. And now, when you gaze at the stately ruins of a lost civilization in Teotihuacán, Mexico, you may also view the future ruins of a contemporary culture from atop the ancient Pyramid of the Sun. In the parking lot of the Wal-Mart being built near the two-thousand-year-old city the Aztecs later found and called the Place Where Men Become Gods, a small pre-Hispanic altar recently unearthed will sit for the rest of eternity under Plexiglas.

We cannot catalog all that has been lost. Even the stars.

Going back to vanished history, people have been reading pictures in the sky. Children of the modern age, children of the fifties who were of tenderly impressionable years and thus are haunted still by seeing Daddy aim the camera at a small screen to capture something hitherto unimagined—*he climbed down the ladder and put his foot on another world*—would look and look at the dark canopy of stars until their brains reeled with the possibilities. *Lost in Space* was a real option. But now the Milky Way is no more. Or rather, if it exists but no one can see it, does it still bloom with mysterious light? According to a report by Italian astronomers, more than two thirds of Americans and more than one half of Europeans can no longer see with the naked eye the galaxy to which the earth belongs. The lighted tree in the backyard looks so dramatic, doesn't it, and you feel no danger anymore in the dark, do you? Every house with its "security" light, multiplied by millions, joined by billions of streetlights, office lights, parking-lot lights, bridge lights, headlights; it's called light pollution, caused by reflection on particles of water vapor and dust motes (of which there are more and more, courtesy of what might be called "the Other Pollution"). A British astronomer notes, "You would have been able to see the Milky Way every clear night for the past 5 million years, and now people have taken it away from us because they can't aim lights properly. . . . Some of that light has taken millions of years to get here and we snuff it out in the last millisecond of its journey."

Things are different in the daytime, too. Have you noticed just how hot the sun feels on your hair these days? It is no life giver, worship idol, without which we would be lost in cold, dead worlds. It is something that disseminates poison into our skin. The sun will just about kill us if we stay in its presence for very long: "From 10 to 2 no sun for you!" runs the rhyme in the state health-department pamphlets for children, decrying the hours of greatest peril. Yes, our kiddies may still run around in the light of day. But first they must have their hazmat suits on. It is a perilous world indeed.

THERE ARE YET *nice* things in New Jersey. When everything that was originally there was combed from the map, there rose on the prepared beds of concrete something that looked very much like . . . like what had been there before! This then is the state's great contribution to mankind: the creation of simulacra so appealing in cleanliness, accessibility, manageability, that the whole world has taken notice and followed suit. I will not be so pedestrian as to cite examples that actually exist *in* New Jersey; instead I will pontificate on the consummate New Jersey*ness* of preferring the nature we make to the nature that just happened to be here first. From the smallest item—the rock that is no mere accident of geology but is rather an example of applied industry, amalgamated from rock dust and other superior ingredients and preformed for uniform shape and ease of use—to the largest—a sandy-beached, bepalmed island in the Caribbean put there by a cruise line—we can do it better. We can make a vast carpet of green in the desert and put little holes in it to make the people come and the insects and extraneous growing things go. These places of recreation and appreciation for the great outdoors are something of a championship trophy for humankind. There is no country that couldn't stand to have a few hundred more golf courses. Even Japan, with a total land area nearly as big as California, has 1,700 and still needs more. Thus there are over three hundred newly built or currently under construction in that country—and one thousand more being considered. Biodiversity, schmiodiversity, say the patrons of these lush playgrounds, who don't mind the nitrogen in the soil one little bit. There's an emerald color you just can't get anywhere else.

For some time now we have accepted the solace of simulated habitats so that we are not unduly disturbed when we visit the zoo. The old bare concrete cells and square blue pools have been dressed up with extruded rock and polyethylene greenery and free-form shapes and synthetic, dyed soil. Fool the eye, fool the mind. Fool the ethics.

We are now ready to move on to the habitat of the favored species.

In the ads the new hometowns look as alluring as the old ones, except that there aren't many old ones like them left, and they were certainly never as perfect. The architects' renderings are done with watercolor, to get the lovely blue blur in the sky over the almost pointillist green-and-olive shrubbery that mysteri-ously bloomed to full height in a single morning. Some gray is dissipating in the face of that blue—the sunset is going to make itself seen after all—with the added value of rain-slicked streets that gaily reflect the theater marquee's lights and the people flocking down the sidewalks. (*People on sidewalks . . .*) The build-ings are all of slightly differing profiles and materials, although one might notice that these differences are repeated precisely in the next block, and the one after that. Forward-thinking towns, or at least forward-thinking developers in them, are these days aiming the wrecking ball at outmoded malls and erecting *commu-nities* in their places. These uniformly have, among other ele-ments, a village green; gazebo bandstand; meetinghouse; sidewalk cafés; greensward; strict regulations on where cars should be hidden. Their house lots are offered to anyone—just plain people!—as "the last remaining pieces of a dream"; a "new hometown"; "the spirit and lifestyle of a real hometown," for once truthfully if inadvertently admitting that real is the last thing it is. The most important "amenities" tendered by these new places in which to sink roots are *stores*, so many you might be forgiven for thinking this is not much different than the strip mall it replaced. These are not just any stores, though; they are the ones you have come to know and trust, the ones that are everywhere else. You can even buy a deluxe loft apartment above one. And won't you be the envy of all your friends to inhabit a veritable landmark like Williams-Sonoma. It is a fundamentally imponderable question of the cosmic variety which came first, the need to build houses near stores or the need to build stores near houses.

It is less mind-bending to wonder what might be the effect on a child of growing up amid, gazing at, absorbing through the very skin these things whose main property is that they look like other, actually genuine things. Surely you can tell in a second, if only by the most amorphous of senses, what is fake and what is not. Laminate wears its falseness on its sleeve; sod in no way exudes true grassness. Mercury vapor is not like moonlight, and a stage set built to look like a New England village is not a village in New England. But still, don't you have some suspicion that if one grows up smelling polyester-silk bouquets, that is what will come to seem fragrant?

So many revelations appear these days when driving. One is that there is much space yet left in central Pennsylvania, and that is where you might go if things continue where you are. The long green sight lines along I-80 outlast the valiantly excessive speed you are putting on to get from one distant place to another, this state the only thing between the two. Come around a long sweeper of a curve, and new vistas of forest spread out below and above, putting you in their embrace. Then another one, but here there is suddenly something wrong. On the top of a ridge is a sight so hideous, so wantonly deviant, it actually causes your heart to start beating fast. A strange fear (you do not yet know of what) washes through you. It feels so primal you might as well be facing Godzilla, a monster you have never seen but know in every cell you must oppose. It is a tree, but it is not a tree. It is fully five times the height of the other trees around it, and its branches are also like claws but bent at forty-five-degree angles with a regularity nature rarely attains. You are going so fast now, adrenaline adding to the velocity of your car, you must turn your head several times lest it recede before you know what to make of this horrible apparition. Who has put it there, and for what nefarious use?

Oh, god, do they take us for idiots?

THE COLLEGE WE were lately sprung from saw fit to give the dear friend its major postgraduate art award, for the monumental and rigorous abstract paintings she made in the nether reaches of Hoboken's warehouse district, hard by what she dubbed the Burma Road—cars on it heading for the Holland Tunnel bounced gingerly in and out of potholes the size of tires. We celebrated with dinner together at the famous Clam Broth House, which opened in 1899 and seemed like it must have been heading resolutely downhill ever since, though history actually records many decades of reasonably edible food and uncountable happy patrons lured by the giant pointing hand on the roof lined with classic neon. We may or may not have gotten mild food poisoning on that occasion; it was possibly a later visit. Anyway, suddenly several thousand dollars richer, she paid for whatever it was we ate and drank. This in itself felt exciting. It seemed to promise future occasions of abandon in recognition of great achievements. Now "life" was about to begin! The opening credits had at long last stopped rolling. What I didn't know was that, yes, life would now be unreeling, but it wasn't going to contain me.

This was the age, and therefore the place, for friendships that exceeded at times the ferocious energy of those first hormonal loves. For a moment it had seemed like our fates were as bound together as our days: we lived together, ate together, went on drives and to parties together, spoke of art and politics and future wishes together. And then one night she did not come home. Or the next. Two days later she stopped by to pick up some clothes. The next week she arrived in the presence of a person who had been my only other close friend, and so he and she were lost to me in a single blow.

It is not possible at this remove to recapture what happened in the next few months. The time was shredded by some sort of frenzy and does not now exist in memory. But at the end of it was a new apartment, just down the block. (I was like those about whom a clever friend once quipped, upon seeing a village in New York named New Kingston about forty miles west of Kingston, "Those must have been some goddamn lazy pioneers.") The nineteenth-century tenement house was identical to the one I had left in such bitterness. The apartment, though, was on the top floor and came with a new roommate. We painted the plywood subflooring of the central room a lovely aqua blue and called it the floor. The kitchen was a cubbyhole punched out of the side of this room, which never contained much furniture and did not have the space for it anyway. We put no curtains on the new metal-frame windows, and in winter the steel gray of the view outside became of a piece with the chill of the empty air inside. For one year I had the use of a charming, large bedroom with a mantelpiece and tile-faced fireplace, albeit unworking. Then it was time to trade. The other room was big enough only for a single bed, which I guess didn't matter, until it did. I unheedingly put matchstick blinds on the window. After living in this room for three months, I got a message from someone on the street to tell that girl on the top floor I can see everything that goes on in her room.

The next place was one block farther back, making me think I had escaped from Bloomfield Street and thus from misery. The move to Garden Street was undertaken in the blush of a first true love, and it did seem as incredible and unlikely then as it does now. I was in need of the privacy of my own apartment, and the absence of a roommate was the salient feature of the new place that made me unable to see any deficits whatever. I had leisure to repent my sightlessness later. Though it was immediately evident that the brown Masonite walls required white paint, I was oblivious to the true nature of these three rooms.

And so I remained for some time, since I spent more of my time in an equally small but infinitely cheerier apartment in downtown Brooklyn. In those days, in that situation, one's apartment was hardly the point. Neither, exactly, was the job in publishing. We were only nominally at work during the day, passing notes, reading short stories, checking the nightlife listings in the *Voice*, talking on the telephone, and typing our poetry on the Selectric. We sent it to each other via interoffice mail. We stayed late in order to impress our bosses, and to make some headway on the slush pile of manuscripts that was delivered daily to us by a silver mail cart creaking under the weight of them. We stayed late because it felt exciting to do so, and because when we left the office the last streaks of pink in the sky had given way to the black velvet of the night canopy that was always held up by the illuminated columns of Manhattan's breathless architecture. We knew where to go; we drank our wine free at art openings in SoHo, and we actually looked at the art, too. The roving clubs with no addresses did not disdain us. We borrowed cars and took trips to the wilds upstate. We rode the subway to the last stop at Coney Island and debarked to spend a winter day on the beach. Sleep was for Sunday mornings.

Yet somewhere behind the scenery the threads were coming undone. Now you would say: of course—how could it last? But then you did not know this was the way it was always going to end. It was something you did, or something you were, far underneath your professed desire for happiness, goodness and kindness, success. The backdrops started sagging; then the ropes gave way. There was one moment where it seemed there was beauty wherever you looked, then suddenly another when you were alone in the apartment on Garden Street, and it revealed itself to you.

The dreams began, grew, magnified themselves in insistence and grandeur and detail until they were realer than the days. You longed for the time to sleep, because then you were delivered to their precincts. You were dreaming of space. Great halls of space underneath the place you lived. Look! A Moroccan-tile swimming pool in an echoing room just below your apartment. Or beside: enter the little dark closet under the staircase, where the dust rained down on your clothes every time the other tenants walked upstairs, and there was a secret doorway onto a magnificent house. Why, it must belong to you, since its only access was through your apartment! It had been closed up for so long, waiting, its deep green velvet drapes pooled on the floor, its overstuffed armchairs and wall sconces and oriental rugs and high ceilings all yours on the other side of an enormous kitchen, and French doors opening onto a flagstone terrace collecting the fallen leaves of an ancient shade tree. The labyrinthine, hidden places of your dreams became the Russian novel you wanted never to end.

Because you now realized you had willingly entered your prison. It was dark, filthy beyond reckoning, and so small it was not possible to take a full breath. And it was overrun with mice. You heard them in the kitchen, a darkly crusted-over place you assiduously avoided, all night long. Then, because your bed was next to it, in a lightless dungeon so cramped it permitted only that single piece of furniture, you heard them under the futon's platform. You began to see evidence of them in your bed, on your dining table, in your bookshelves. You became so distracted you forgot you had signed a pact of nonviolence and began to kill them by the score with still no diminution of their presence. With your rent check, you started to send the landlord a monthly death count. He did not particularly care for this. His displeasure might have had more of an impact were he not the editor in chief of *Newsweek*, and thus the recipient of a paycheck the size of which you could only guess, and the inhabitant of a four-story brownstone ten blocks uptown that was every bit as elegant as the place you believed you deserved. You started to sleep with the lights on—or tried to sleep anyway—in the mistaken belief that this would at least keep the mice away from your sheets.

You had made another grave error and left work, at which you had spent two and a half years without advancing past the entry-level position, for university. Your soul mate had departed, naturally, for a better university in another state. So now you were truly alone, without even the unwanted attentions of the mail-room worker who gave you that Christmas present out of the blue. You spent three hours every day on the PATH and the subway to go to a place where you never befriended a single classmate or communicated with any but strangely hostile professors. At least you had Mary Tyler Moore in late-night reruns on the tiny black-and-white television your parents had given you, a gift that caused you to weep in a swollen admixture of unnameable emotions.

Finally you admitted defeat and slunk out into the springtime not a free woman but freed from at least one dream. You were not meant for that life. You were not meant for any, it seemed, and the small apartment grew smaller, its dinginess dingier. The summer bloomed, and on Garden Street it was as gray as it ever was, only hotter. The basement apartment in the next building spilled forth its changing mixture of tenants, at its center an undigested lump of dough-white flesh in a wispy housecoat with nothing else underneath. She sat outside your window all day, holding a broomstick with which to occasionally beat her emaciated German shepherd in a burst of yelling that resembled spoken English only tangentially. Other equally preternaturally white people went in and out, along with more naturally tinted individuals who spoke Spanish. They were as unlikely a cohabiting group as the fact that apparently the Appalachians had come to Hoboken. Why? Weren't things bad enough at home? Someone later gave you the answer: New Jersey's cranberry farms imported pickers from West Virginia and when the harvest was in, they decided to stay. That also explained the ancient pickup truck permanently parked under an overpass on the Burma Road, home to an entire family of these strangely white specimens.

Until the largesse once more of your parents—your mother sat down on the tiny love seat and wept the first time she visited your apartment—provided a small air conditioner that did not cool so much as make white noise, these people outside inhabited your rooms as well. Their incessant arguing circled your brain along with the words of the paperback romance novel you were supposed to copyedit, or of the movie review you were to write for the *Hoboken Reporter* in order to get twenty-five dollars. One day of the week you were spared this auditory imprisonment because of the one good thing in your current life, courtesy of Time-Life's union and their bottomless basket of plums. In exchange for getting paid to stay up all night once per week to read the occasional article for errors in spelling, grammar, sense, and computer coding, you got to use the rest of the time to make long-distance calls, read books and newspapers, joke around with the other proofreaders, pocket the dinner money, and emerge from the Lincoln Tunnel in a Town Car just as pink overspread the Hudson County sky. Then you could enter the lightless lair that was your bedroom and pull the blanket over your head and sleep until three, and miss almost an entire day of pointless wrangling by the people just outside your window who were beginning to install fantasies in your head of brutal mishaps and terrible upshots that might occur to a group of unrelated (or overrelated) malingerers.

One morning you had just put down your bag on the table in the front room and started to take off your shoes when a strange but almost beautiful sound began filling the apartment. At first it was not possible to determine whence it came: the closet under the stairs? It sounded like an Amazonian waterfall, and that would be the logical place for such a phantom to hide itself. As you entered the no-man's-land of the kitchen, though, the source of the music appeared through the back window. Money was falling past. The sound of copper and silver as it plinged against the fire escape and hit the concrete of the backyard enriched the air. The coins kept raining. Stranger things had happened in Hoboken, surely, but they had never happened to you. Only the solid sense that reality simply never provided for occurrences of magical profit, gained slowly over the past four years, prevented you from putting your cupped hands out the window.

All will be revealed in the light of a Hoboken day. And so it was that some local lowlifes, having expended all their intelligence in casing the building and determining that the nice young couple on the top floor for some inscrutable reason left home every day by the early-morning rush, attempted to make away with their loose change. It was stored in a twenty-five-gallon glass water jar. And it was a bloody idiotic thing to try to get out of a window and down a fire escape. Thus went all instances of enchantment in the place that defined disappointment.

On Washington Street (what wasn't on Washington Street? That is, except for the obscenely delicious focaccia hot out of the oven at Marie's bakery, and the live chickens clucking as if their lives depended on it somewhere farther down Second Street, and the fried ravioli at the shrine to native son Frank Sinatra that was only incidentally a restaurant named, truly, Leo's Grandevous, on Grand Street) was an ostensibly Mexican eatery called East L.A. It was actually a private club for all those who could outwait the Saturday-morning line. And because it was pretty much the only place one could get that newfangled thing called brunch—aka breakfast for anyone who had been to Maxwell's the night before—a familiar cast of characters populated the booths every weekend. Occasionally the waitstaff changed faces. And so it was that the girl who brought the huevos rancheros one day was different. Very different. She stopped after sliding the plate across the booth table and announced she knew you. You had gone to the same college. And on this flimsy pretext the projector once more whirred into action, and the teeth in the sprockets pulled life on.

She had what they call raven hair, though that did not really qualify its ability to sum her up: deep, reverberating, a quasar in the center of the universe, or at least the constellations above a very small town. Once she had taken you in—plucked you up off the sidewalk, why you did not know, only she saw something redeemable there and set out to redeem it—you, too, became a sort of center, so long as you stood by her. The bartender at Maxwell's, previously just another attractive woman with enviable self-possession and the connections that go with it, became a friend, because she was a friend of hers. No more standing in line. No more standing out in the cold. No more waiting—for anything. She swept you away to a parallel world of parties, people *with potential*, even the possibility of a future not devoid of love. Neither of you would voice the reality that, for now, men were beside the point. The two of you were as large as figures on a billboard towering over the approach to the tunnel, blocking even the sun. There was joy for you again, and the two of you went everywhere, taking photographs, talking about the movies you wanted to make, haunting the basement junk shops. You gave each other presents. You conferred about plans. She was the first person you had ever known to paint her bedroom bloodred, and such boldness floored you.

There was nothing she could not do. Keep a boyfriend, well . . . who could? But she cemented her status as wizard the morning she called and asked if you were dressed. If not, get your clothes on quick, and go back to Jefferson Street, number 114. If no one's there, go back a few doors, and you'll see a storefront office; my friend's a lawyer and his girlfriend's a filmmaker. They can tell you how to get in to see the apartment.

Okay, so it was in the back of beyond, that strange tangle of statesmen's names that kept changing order as you went down First Street, which you had actually never done. Damn, but it was far. From Garden, cross Park, Willow, Clinton, Grand, Adams— though who knew, since most of the original blue enamel street signs, tacked to buildings, had long ago been lost. It was a solid twenty-minute walk from the PATH train—but it was a place to live. Not a wretched den, not filled with the odor of rodents, not a place that made you long to leave it with such a fierceness it almost made you sick, but a real apartment with light, and one whole story above street level. Across from it were not the identical tenements there used to be: now there were single-family houses, of new brick, just like in the suburbs; they were either public-access housing or private-connection housing. They had bay windows that in December would be filled with spangled cotton batting and lighted miniature scenes of a happy long ago that never existed but that made you want to inhabit them with all the sentiment you outwardly disdained but inwardly bathed in.

The one thing the apartment didn't have was heat. If it had been advertised in the *Reporter* or the window of a Washington Street realtor, it would have been advertised as "gas-on-gas," but since you had no idea what this meant it could hardly have changed anything. You had certainly come across the notion of a cold-water flat in various works of literature, but it was not until much later that you learned that they existed on this continent. You had made a deal with an older Italian-American man to pay cash for the privilege of living in one.

What it did have was a peculiar gas stove, with an open grille in the side. This, you learned somewhere around the end of October, was the heat. The apartment was fully twice the size of your previous one, though still a railroad. So while you felt nice and cozy warm with your belly pressed up against the side of the stove, with your cat purring on the top of it and a book propped against her back, it would not do to place a chair and sit right next to it. Too far away.

And in the mornings you woke to the sight of your own breath crystallizing like a halo above you, or like the tangible residue of your impossible dreams. The wall, as thin as all the rest in this hastily built town, could not be touched without mittens. But she, *she*, had helped you paint it. The floor became the gentlest pink the eye could discern. The whole thing seemed to hover in lightness. You could not believe your good fortune. For something had been happening in Hoboken, and apartments were not easy to find. Your eye recast this one as spare, modernist, even though what it was was about twice as good as the former one, and we know how good that was. It was also the beginning of the end, and the beginning of a new beginning.

Your year was almost up. You had no way to know it, but she only gave about twelve months. Twelve months in the blinding shine of the footlights, then once more hooked off the stage. She had quietly found someone else, and they were even now researching each other. With excitement, they learned that their hearts beat with the same rhythm. She repainted her bedroom because she was bored with it, but you never saw that next color.

The walks to Maxwell's took on a desperate edge: it seemed not possible to be farther away from the place and still be in the same town. At one or two in the morning, alone after being alone in the midst of a crowd, walking through the empty streetscape in the cold dark, Hoboken once more bled into your blood. For nearly an hour you walked, and the thought came and sat on your shoulder, leaving its droppings there: you would never get out of here. "Here" meant your wretched state of mind at one and the same with a wretched state.

To show how debased you had become, the opening of Quick Check on Washington and Second was cause for celebration in your small heart. It was like a Cumberland Farms had been picked up whole from a suburban parking lot and parachuted here. But it was new, it was clean, and it was carpeted. Most of all, it was open until midnight, thus open six hours past everyplace else, and that felt promising. It was like hearing the phone ring: see, someone wants to *talk* to *me*. After working all day alone in your apartment, finally at dusk shelving the hope that an editor was going to return your calls, you would offer yourself a consolation prize: a trip to Quick Check. You would wander around, in the company of other humans, and finally settle on a Hershey bar, a fat copy of *Vogue*, and, from the plastic tub near the cash register, a bouquet of chrysanthemums and carnations. Then back to Jefferson Street, carrying the items that would enable you to temporarily forget where you were. Quick Check kept you alive, and if anyone knew that, you'd just die.

Life had not been unequivocally bad; it was just that you tended to forget the little triumphs that bobbed like corks in the sea of despair. Narcissism is one of the toughest maladies to cure. There had been many awkward gropings with wayward objects of lust or boredom: perhaps other people knew how to have amazing, video-ready tussles in bed with someone they had just met the week before, but you had yet to figure out how, and so did the unfortunates you were repeatedly drawn to. Somewhat more brightly, you were managing to put together a living from a patchwork of freelance work: there was no publication, however unreadable, however unread, to which you would not agree to contribute. You also drank deeply from the teats of the Time-Life cash cow. And something, like a sunrise, was massing on the horizon. It would soon shine on you, and on its rays you would walk up and away from Hoboken forever.

BETWEEN 1978 AND 1982, fifty-six people, most of them children, died in highly suspicious tenement fires in Hoboken. The majority of these presumed arsons were never prosecuted. The sky blazed red at night, and the smell of burned things persisted through the days. Soon there was not a block in the whole town on which roll-off containers did not take up parking spaces; a whizzing could be heard from every other building as interior debris slid down the chutes from upper-story windows. In five years, one fifth of all the rental housing stock in town had been converted to condos and, no matter their provenance or their size, were declared to be "luxury." Real-estate offices appeared like mushrooms in a wet woods. National media proclaimed a boom in a city whose very name used to cause muffled laughter. Apartments that had previously gone begging—as well they might, having in the seventies ranked the worst in the northeast, half with substandard plumbing, most without central heat—were recast as appealing lodgings for employees of Wall Street.

The problem was that the people who had clung to these apartments for better and for worse, through decades of neglect, were now an impediment to their marvelous transformation. Hence the flames in the night. The artists were smart enough to leave with a few choice words tossed over their shoulders, and then the factories and warehouses were on their way to becoming "luxury" lofts. But the Hispanic and Italian families, many children strong, did not know where to go next. Their indecisiveness was, to the developers, hard to tolerate. The offer of a few hundred dollars could not persuade them to leave, especially since there was nowhere else a few hundred dollars could begin to purchase a home in which to live.

The town erupted in a sort of civil war, only the fusillades of musket fire were heard as vitriol in the letters to the editor of the *Hoboken Reporter*. It was a better venue than a voting booth, with no electoral college or graft or insincere speech making to prevent a voice from being heard: every letter was printed essentially as received. Some people had missed their true calling. The slurs, names, and extended metaphors were lobbed back and forth with increasing animosity and literary brio between the forces of the newcomer Yuppies and the B and R's—those "born and raised" in Hoboken. One event that emblematized the trouble was the church-sponsored Feast of the Madonna dei Martiri, which over the course of nine days each year shrouded much of Hoboken in blue smoke and left pets and citizens shaking from the effect of blocklong strings of fireworks and "feast bombs" detonated from cannons. This made many, many newcomers angry, which caused most of the city's Italian Americans to get very angry in return. Quoth both sides: How dare they?

But shouting, or long screeds that shouted in print, mattered as much as the black graffiti scrawled on every developer's sign: THIS IS DISPLACEMENT; CONDOS SUCK; YUPPIE GO HOME. They mattered not one bit. Hoboken was not changing so much as being eradicated, then reborn as something else. They kept only the name the same.

IT WAS THE KIND of perfect fall day where the air itself feels energized, the forces of vanishing warmth and incoming cold tensely balanced. I did not know where I was. This was a charming place. There were young trees up and down every street; people had planted dooryard gardens and cheerful window boxes. It reminded me a little of Nantucket. Trim young women wheeled expensive prams along the main street, past stores selling triple-milled soaps and clever children's clothes. There were "off-leash" dogs gamboling in the parks, not just off-leash dogs. Every restaurant, and there were so many, had tables out in sidewalk cafés, with French-inflected advertising umbrellas protecting the healthy complexion of the handsome diners underneath. The many nightspots waited silently for later.

Then I stopped, and whirled around. I do not know how the truth had come to me, for there was no outward sign, but I knew. I knew where I was.

The only greenery I had seen a long time ago was the "garden" of the old Italian man in the apartment downstairs: three fig trees wrapped up with burlap in the cold. How I used to fantasize that he would die quietly in his sleep one night, and then I could have his flat: I would get a dog and a garden bench, or at least leave the door open for a breeze. Nothing can express the barrenness of the view of that frozen backyard.

Now it was situated in the midst of ripe fullness. There were no gaping cracks anymore. There were no abandoned streets. No forgotten parks. No withered branch on which despair could alight, cawing and cawing until you put your hands over your ears and screamed, *Enough! Lord, please, enough.*

And this felt bizarrely sad. At least it had been my despair, and very, very real.

Fabian's Brauhaus had been a bar at First and Bloomfield, a remnant of the day when Hoboken was reputed to have more bars per capita than any other city in the nation. It had remained essentially unchanged from the time when all life in Hoboken was like it was in *On the Waterfront*, or only as many blocks back from the wharves as the sailors and longshoremen could stagger. The only things different about Fabian's thirty years later were that they had closed its back room because there was no longer the need for so many tables to serve the hordes of customers, as there were no hordes of customers, and that the paintings on the walls had taken on a gorgeous yellow patina of age. Otherwise it was the greatest place in the whole world, the payoff that almost made living in that town worthwhile. A couple of old-timers sat at the bar every night, while a few of those promising new faces quietly talked at tables. The light of the jukebox spilling soft colors on the page was enough to write by.

First it became Cryan's Exchange—a stockbroker's theme bar. The old paintings were gone, because they were dingy and did not fit the concept. After that it became McSwiggans, a jazzed-up fake Irish pub, to join the sixty-seven other fake Irish pubs that now marched up and down Hoboken's streets and invited frat boys to drink enough fake Irish beer to float the whole town away on their vomit.

Aversa's Market on First Street had been there since the first Italian immigrants had ridden boats and trolleys on their way from Ellis Island. Even if you had no common language the stern shop men were able to tell you with their eyes that you were not to touch their produce; they would do that. Two pounds of pears, a bunch of arugula, and a ball of fresh mozzarella? It was selected for you and placed into paper bags that were folded over and held in one hand while the other figured the total on the flat surface of the brown paper with a short pencil wet periodically on the tongue. Your money would disappear into an ornate gold cash register with tall keys that each rang a bell when depressed. The fruits and vegetables might have come out of a Caravaggio.

Now the windows of Aversa's were blacked out and bore a sign informing that it was soon to become the Weary Epicurean: "Finest Food Since You Ate at Grandma's House." No, no, the finest food was at *Aversa's*.

Who thought this stuff up? *Do they take us for idiots?* Hoboken had become Luxuryland, a subsidiary of Disney. In addition to the fake Irish bars, there were fake manufacturing lofts—made-up squalor itself remade, only the whole fiction arose at once on a vacant lot. There were fake English mews with a Tudor look, but they were actually parking garages for a few of the billions of vehicles that so choked Hoboken's streets it had become impossible to park within half a mile of a destination. A developer called the building he intended to build on the site of the Maxwell House coffee plant a "condominium concept." You pay extra for those over just plain condos; this one is intended to go for five hundred dollars per square foot. Already the town has been improved with condo buildings whose concepts included not only workout rooms but putting greens. For the first time since 1950, Hoboken put on weight: the 2000 census revealed a population burst of 15 percent. Slowboken no longer, eh?

This future was, of course, foretold. I was happy the day they opened a health-food store called Hoboken Farmboy, so I had somewhere to get my granola, but I should have known. The bigger tip-off was the foundation of the Hoboken Historical Museum in 1988, because the "living history" stuff is all over by the point at which they conceive the inauguration of dead exhibits. They are necessary when the past is no longer visible in the present.

The place I knew is gone; the place that retained history's marks is gone. In its place are cigar bars and martini bars. The hippie café—I can still taste the tahini dressing on the sprout-and-sunflower-seed salad—that offered a quiet table for hours for the price of a cup of mint tea is now a place called Whiskey Bar. And Maxwell's came very close to dying in the nineties when a new owner tried to turn it into a microbrew pub. These things are weirdly stunning; they dislocate you from everything you know and toss you into a world where nothing makes sense, not even the fact that such trivialities as these nonetheless feel important, as if they are trying to tell you something but can't. They seem to be asking you to look for something you left in your past, maybe something that dropped through a hole in your pocket and was never missed until now. They ask you to retrace your steps and find it, find it, somehow.

I didn't realize then that the lonely wind, which on my long and unhappy walks I leaned into and that blew the tail of my father's heavy coat out behind me as if for ballast, was an eerie wind from long ago. Now, in the placid windless Hoboken of today, my youth gone as well as that persistent unhappiness and its marriage to this place, I missed its brutal insistence that it had something to say about my age and about how to live in the world, my home.

Still, maybe this was meant to be. You cannot stop progress, after all. Perhaps I had to leave it, and then Hoboken could transform itself. Within minutes after my departure, although I did not look back for several years during which my own transformation was being attempted, she had changed her clothes, put on sheer stockings, done her makeup with a sure and suddenly educated hand. If it did not sound so absurdly self-centered, I would have to say the city was waiting for the sound of my door closing for the last time to start getting happy. Maybe it was not Hoboken that dragged me down after all; maybe it was I who kept Hoboken from achieving its true potential.

In *The American Scene*, Henry James wrote, "it was an adventure, unmistakably, to have a revelation made so convenient—to be learning at last, in the maturity of one's powers, what New Jersey might 'connote.'" The place I hated is gone. The place I apparently loved also is gone. My convenient revelation was that there is not to be any revelation, only a sickening coating of irony dripping from the whole experience. "New Jersey" connoted altogether too much: desperate desires, the whitewash of memory, the realization that everything I then wanted to throw away as fast as I could with both hands is what I am now woozy with loss over. I would give anything to again walk down one of those desolate streets at night (the cold without an echo of the unhappiness within). Because when I reached my goal at last, I would be filled with hope, that everything was about to change.

NOTES

Hanging on the exposed brick: The painting was by Tim Daly.

Indeed, it was a good time: A little later, one of the best of the Hoboken bands formed out of northeastern talent: Yo La Tengo.

We lived in Hudson County: By 1960, the population density of the state was eight hundred people per square mile, the highest in the United States. And I'd always heard that Hoboken was once the most thickly settled city in the country, although not by the time I moved to its depopulated precincts. The extraordinary density extended to the state's garbage as well, as noted by Peter C. Jones in *The Changing Face of America*: "In 1989 the New Jersey shoreline averaged 300,000 pounds of trash per mile, compared with the national average of 3,000 pounds of trash per mile. Much of the debris seems to come from crumbling decks and piers, remnants of once-thriving ports."

"Crisscrossed by railroads": Kevin Lynch, *The Image of the City*, 1960.

Cadillac Escalades and eight-bedroom "homes": You have noticed this is the second time "homes" appears within quotes; a quick perusal of real estate advertised by any demonstrably tony agency will educate one to the fact that, when it is for sale, it is not a house, it is a *home*.

Since 1970 average American families: The source for this is the National Association of Home Builders, who ought to be ashamed of themselves.

In the twenties: From the essay titled "New Jersey: The Slave of Two Cities," commissioned from Edmund Wilson by *The Nation* and published in a two-volume collection, *These United States: Portrait of America from the 1920s*. Later, the writer Luc Sante was asked by *The Nation* to treat his view of Jersey for an updated *These United States* published in 2003.

$350 billion per year: Oh, those monumental numbers again!

the Supercenters can fill 220,000 square feet: Ditto.

A British astronomer notes: *The Guardian Weekly*, October 9–15, 2003.

"the last remaining pieces"; *"new hometown"*; *"the spirit and lifestyle"*: Seaside, Florida; Arverne by the Sea, Rockaway, New York; and Traditions at Historic Southbury[!], Connecticut, respectively.

every letter was printed essentially as received: Four years' worth of these letters were collected in the book *Yuppies Invade My House at Dinnertime: A Tale of Brunch, Bombs, and Gentrification in an American City*, 1987, edited by Joseph Barry and John Derevlany. It is as riveting as a well-made novel.

HOME FIRES, BURNING

Here I was at the end of America—no more land—and
now there was nowhere to go but back.

—KEROUAC, *On the Road*

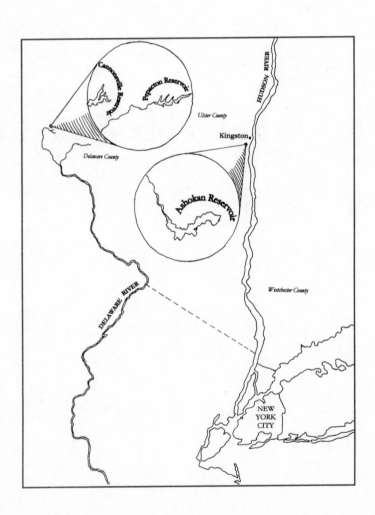

THE CAR IS traveling on a roadway strung along the edge of a placid blue lake that is endless. Then you say brightly, *Did you know that when the water gets low, the tips of the church steeples emerge and soon the lost towns rise up from their graves?* and the dark imagination takes the image, runs away. In that moment it becomes as unremovable from the brain as if it had been utterly true, and not a concoction of popular fable that just will not die, made as it is for the susceptible person who, in the middle of life, finds all homes slipping away as if into water.

IT IS NOT EVEN the capital of New York State, but New York City is now thought of as the capital of the world, at least by its residents. It is a magnificent, unprecedented, teeming place. For those who admire the works of man, a miracle.

It came from water. Here is just the beginning: In 1799, the ever-growing town on the isle of Manhattan built a 550,000-gallon reservoir on Chambers Street to attempt to meet its need for potable water, along with six miles of wooden mains and a well. There had been some trouble finding ample springs, and surface sources were often polluted beyond reason; even the horses would go without rather than drink their output. Yellow fever and other waterborne diseases made constant rounds of the populace. Fire, too, was insatiably thirsty, and with its need unmet threatened to destroy the closely built wooden structures of the town in a heart-stoppingly short time. And so, in 1837, the city began work on a dam of the Croton River to the north, in order to create a 400-acre reservoir, and 41 and a half miles of aqueduct to get its water down to where it was wanted. Barely had the crews put down their shovels than they had to lift them again: a reservoir covering 96 acres in what would become Central Park was started in 1858. But wait. Eight years later the city is going north again to further dam the Croton, this time the West Branch. In another four years the city's population will reach 942,000 people who clamor for 77 million gallons of water per day.

We are 65 percent water, as you learned in school many years ago and never forgot. In the coming 44 years, New York City was to condemn 8,300 acres of land it did not own in order to provide the water its citizens required. In Putnam County, the old villages of Southeast Center, Milltown, Farmers Mills, and Red Mills vanished: houses and hotels and barns and slaughterhouses and privies and pigsties along the banks of lakes and streams were condemned, the owners allowed to buy them back at auction for a couple of dollars and move them to higher ground. Or else.

Another fifty thousand people were added to the city's population rolls when it annexed the villages of Morrisania, Kingsbridge, and West Farms to what is now the Bronx, with a predictable outcome for the upstate village of Kensico. Its inhabitants were forced to disperse so their places might be drowned by a reservoir that would store 1,797,000 gallons of water. In 1890 the population of the great city was 1.4 million, and they used 145 million gallons per day. Five years later, though, it amounted to 165 million gallons of water per day. (You know by now this is not the end.)

It sounds like desiccated ancient history: *the villages were drowned*. Yes, and what am I supposed to think? There is only so much I can feel for people long ago, talked about in a book.

Perhaps, then, you might move to a new home. There, down at the end of your winding, rutted, often wild road, past the mobile homes and the stone houses and white frame buildings with simple porches and the new weekend places set on old land with stone walls receding into the creeping woods, you would discover a place of surpassing strangeness. The pine forest to both sides of the well-surfaced road is like a thick curtain against something—certainly the sun, but also against something else. It is dark and confusing, and you can rarely tell which way to go when the road forks. There is a uniformity to the view that does not seem exactly natural. Maybe it's a park. But no; wire fencing to keep you out extends to the end of sight. White signs are posted on every other segment of it. NEW YORK CITY WATER SUPPLY / NO TRESPASSING. You did not think you were in New York City—rather, you thought you were a hundred miles from it, which was sort of the point—but here you are. The city came and found you.

It came and found many people: people who did not want to be found, who had never even seen that gluttonous place, who had no wish to leave where they were. Then, in their own way, these people came and found you. The queer fate that befell them is what you think about when you look out your own window, toward a landscape that could be transformed, in the ruminating imagination, to a place just like theirs.

The long reach of New York City's grasp rendered more than ten thousand people temporarily homeless, but many felt permanently so for the rest of their days. Most of them moved to the periphery of the center that was no longer available to them, because it had been drowned. There they would daily walk or ride or drive by the body of water that was an unwanted memorial to their lost homes. They received money for their land, but to sell a place that contains your heart is to traffic in blood money. Money does not pay for everything.

WITH THE KIND of loopy fiction magazine writers sometimes come up with to enliven an article's opener, to *draw the reader in*, in 1908 the author of a piece in *Harper's Weekly* strung out a five-years-into-the-future tale of the long-gone traveler returning home from abroad. He tries to buy a ticket to his hometown in upstate's Ulster County but is told by the agent that no such village exists. The man is eager to see the old homestead again and with mounting frustration figures he will take the train to a nearby stop and get to Brodhead's Bridge from there somehow.

By now (if not well before) the reader can pretty much guess what happens, especially since the title of the article is "Submerging Eight Villages in a Drinking Fountain." The only thing the wondering passenger can see out the window is a gigantic blue lake where was once everything he used to know.

Shokan. Brodhead's Bridge. Brown's Station. Olive Bridge. West Hurley. Glenford. Olive. Ashton. (Each one meant to sound as a single toll of the bell.) Gone under the waters. Two thousand people lost their homes. Even the dead lost their homes: considered a contaminant, the residue of human life in those graves was also, to their relations, horrible to contemplate leaving to the fishes. So their remains, in company with what the writer called "every sordid trace" of mammalian occupation of twelve thousand acres that had been settled for more than two hundred years, would have to be scraped from the earth and carted away.

The act of man that caused such godlike meddling with the nature of a portion of the earth was passed by the New York City legislature as chapter 724 of the Laws of 1905 (known as the McClellan Act, after the mayor of the city who was son of the brave

Civil War general). To go back but a sort of minute, the entire business might be also placed in the lap of an unlikely villain, the president of the Manufacturers Association of Brooklyn in 1896. In fact, in no account is he described as doing anything that could remotely be characterized as villainous, but there you go: Charles N. Chadwick was appointed head of a committee to investigate new sources of water for the city that was soon to be a borough. He was a man to think big. Instead of addressing only the current water needs of the great metropolis, he believed they should be settled for no less than fifty years into the future. And since the city was putting on one million new inhabitants with every decade, according to recent history, those needs could not possibly be met with more wells or city reservoirs amounting to rain puddles in the face of a giant's abiding thirst. Chadwick called for the appointment of a board of water commissioners with wide powers to secure the water supply.

And so these pretty pieces of politicking—great and terrible things begin in small, unheeding acts—were responsible not only for the building of the Ashokan Reservoir, which would take these eight small towns and consign them to the bottom of a well, but for the rest of the Catskill System as well. And they were a nice precedent for the further practice of eminent domain farther into the Catskill Mountain region, where in another twenty years the city had a mind to build the Delaware System (and, who knows, might still be mentioned when it takes the first shovelful for the Yukon System). Edward Coykendall, general manager of the Ulster & Delaware Railroad, which would be called upon to rip up and replace many miles of track, called the McClellan "one of the most outrageous acts of confiscation ever passed by a legislature in a civilized country."

But it is never wise to put too much stock in the protestations of someone whose main interest is financial. Listen instead to the penniless, or the homeless. Purdy's Station, moved for the building of the New Croton Reservoir in the last decade of the 1800s, was home to a John Rowe, who in 1899 described the actions that

had taken his village as comprising "the sin of force and greed."
Albert Chamberlain, former citizen of Croton Falls, lamented in
1905, "Money cannot pay for the heartaches and sorrow caused by
being forced to take up a new life among strangers."

It takes heavy equipment to expunge home on such a scale.
And so, to build the embankment on the "north wing, west dike,
and west and middle portions of the middle dike" of the Ashokan
Reservoir, the tally of grave diggers makes a peculiar poem.

2 seventy-ton Bucyrus steam shovels
1 seventy-ton Atlantic steam shovel
1 thirty-ton Atlantic traction shovel
1 thirty-ton Ohio traction shovel
2 Model 20 Marion traction shovels
8 Monarch steam rollers
1 Kelley-Springfield roller
2 Western graders
2 Road machines
2 Buffalo traction engines

Not to mention 64 horses and 365 mules. The sound of the great
construction enterprise drowns out the sound of anything else. It
is deemed astonishing, better than anything since the Roman
aqueducts, since the Panama Canal, and a testament to man's
great powers of—

You have to go search out the file folders of Xeroxed small-
town newspaper articles, and sit reading them by yourself in an
underheated conference room of an historical society. You have
to whisper quietly to the reference librarian. You need to adjust
the headphones of the borrowed tape recorder, or sit down in
front of the jumpy video of an old man speaking in a halting voice.
And that will be all you'll find.

Waving his hand toward the village on the hill he said:
"You Schwonnacks came to this, my home. You entered

our wigwams. By our camp fire we lighted you the pipe of peace. We gave you this land, Waerinnewangh. You dug up the hatchet. You were cowards. . . . You thought we would come back no more. But the dead have called my braves. They are coming. I hear their canoes grate on the pebbles upon the beach. . . . The fires shall sweep away your dwellings. The wolves shall dig in the ashes and the owl hoot among the ruins." . . . Such is the tale as it was told. Its characters were dust and ashes many years ago. The quaint old village has gone forever. . . . All is changed, and yet not all. The Catskills still look down upon the scene. The Esopus still ripples to the sea. The elm, a giant among trees now, still stands, and the night winds whisper among its branches the story of the long ago.

Writing "The Last of the Esopus" in 1896, Augustus H. Van Buren could not have known how truthful, and how false, the words of his fable of the Indians of this region would become. The elm met its own fate. The fires would indeed sweep away the dwellings of the white men who settled on the banks of the Esopus Creek, but they would not have been set in justifiable revenge by the ghosts of the native displaced. That would be the job of the grubbing contractor. And yes, the Esopus would still ripple to the sea—or at least to the Hudson, and thence to New York Harbor—but its path now contained a rude disruption placed there in 1908 near an old landmark at Bishop's Falls. At the picturesque site of the stepped falls was a gristmill and a stone house bearing the date 1796. Here would be the Ashokan's front line, the first place to disappear under water when the 4,650-foot dam—marvel at the longest in the world!—and its attendant weirs, dikes, channels, and conduits were finished. In 1914 a grand signal of completion woke the dead: every steam whistle on the project within twelve square miles blew for one hour straight. The sound meant one thing to the workers, and another to whoever of the two thousand uprooted happened to be within hearing distance. Three years later, a bigger celebration was planned: thousands of the receivers of Nature's largesse, the clear waters of the Esopus born in the mountains of the Catskills and rushing downward one hundred and more miles over rocks and through tunnels and into lakes and under rivers and through pipes, gathered near the old Central Park reservoir. It had begun to receive the water from far north that was needed to augment it almost as soon as it had been built. This event was meant as a sort of thank-you, though it is noticed it did not take place at any of the points of origin of this waylaid wealth. The weather that day had a sense of humor. It rained.

The crowd did not stay to hear all the verse and song meant to laud "The Good Gift of Water." Which was just as well. For how can what is stolen be considered a gift?

THE SIXTIES WERE a good time to rob the Indians, again. Progress, like an armored brigade, had been on the march. There were more and more people—white people, that is—with more and more needs, such as more places to build houses, more electricity to power more and more unnecessary tools that had come to seem necessary, more locales to colonize and in which to pursue activities that had also insinuated themselves into requirement.

In 1964 the Army Corps of Engineers erected a dam to control flooding on the Allegheny River. Two other goals would also be met: pollution abatement and the creation of a pretty lake for "recreation."

The Kinzua Dam buried in water one third of the entire Allegany Indian reservation in western New York and northwest Pennsylvania, to the width of nine thousand acres. These people lost the Cornplanter tract, their last tribal land in Pennsylvania and named for the unfortunate chief who could not see into the future, as well as their spiritual center, the Cold Spring Longhouse. One hundred and thirty families had to move, not for the first time. "In the evenings many continue to wander down to the riverbanks 'to be near where "the old places" used to be,'" says a writer of those who are forced to pine. Another writer, Edmund Wilson, reported in *Upstate: Records and Recollections of Northern New York* that a friend told him about the reservoir: "He made my blood run cold by his account of what was happening to the Seneca Indians as a result of the Kinzua Dam. The Indians or the Quakers who were working for them had consulted a housing expert, who had referred them to some Madison Avenue publicity man. This man had advised them that the only advantageous thing for them was to create an Indian Williamsburg, a replica of an old Indian village."

(This did not in fact come to pass, although if it did it would not have raised a single eyebrow in America after Wilson's estimable one, and it would have been looked on in some quarters as quite an improvement. For we live deep in the heart of a strange territory, one that offers the John Carver Inn, a heady enticement "on the site of the original Pilgrim settlement, featuring 85 rooms including . . . in-room movies. *Pilgrim Cove Indoor Theme Pool* with 80' waterslide, *Mayflower* replica, waterfalls, water cannons. . . . Complete Passport to History Packages available.")

The Canandaigua Treaty of 1794, between the United States and the Iroquois, was a fine treaty, it turned out, and about as trustworthy as all such papers. It gave the Indians who lived from these lands the right to continue "in perpetuity." How short perpetuity can be! Especially when it collides with the desire of more powerful people to take whatever they like, including lives and livelihoods, even if for the most trivial of reasons. And nothing is more trivial than the fixing of three stupid problems—desiring to control the nature of a river; dispose of toxins released by the careless; and have a new place to trailer the fishing boat to—created by greed in the first place.

Still, none of this was murder, since the people would surely scamper away at the last minute to avoid drowning in the rising waters. (Unlike the rabbits in Portugal who died by the thousand when a great dam began to impound water in the Alentejo, starving then drowning as they were pushed up on ever smaller islands that eventually sank beneath the water. But they are of no account.) And the Seneca Nation did accept $15 million, which may be construed as proof that they were compensated.

It is tempting to think that perhaps such an act was really made possible by the unimportance of people who could simply be pushed aside. And technological advancement is working to make it easier all the time. How far away can we go to take what is not ours? Two hundred miles? Two thousand miles? From places where they do not speak our language? From places where they do not know we exist? (Imagine the Togo Islanders arriving on your doorstep to announce they need the topsoil under your house, so it has been condemned. And you just redid the kitchen!)

On the National Trust for Historic Preservation's 2002 list of most endangered places (which will be everyplace, eventually) is "Missouri River Cultural and Sacred Sites," under threat from federal dam and reservoir projects. The organization said these are "destroying Native American burial sites and archeological resources at an alarming rate, even exposing the remains of tribal ancestors." In plain English, their bones are coming up through the earth, emerging along riverbanks. The list's publication was sponsored by Shell Oil.

But no Indians have been as hard done by as the Cree of Quebec. The meddling with ancient rivers that speaks to man's breathtaking hubris, and possibly infantile return to rearranging toy landscapes, took a bold new turn with the James Bay projects of Hydro-Quebec. Phase One alone intended to create seven huge reservoirs (in Quebec's northwest, territory belonging to Cree and Inuit hunter-gatherers) by holding back the waters of five rivers. Four thousand and four hundred square miles of land would be inundated, and nearly 68,000 square miles would be fairly ruined from the unforeseen effects of exploitation, including the spread of methyl mercury. Everything began changing for the Cree. Those who decided to do this enormous thing could not or would not comprehend that what was begun would finish the Cree off: the roads and airports were built first, and they were as pathways for infection. Now there were mines, and cars, and towns full of cheap-built housing, and all manner of foreign things (small ones, like ways of seeing the world, and of living in it) creeping in from the edges. Elements of life began falling like dominoes, for each was placed too closely to the next to stop alone. Journalist Boyce Richardson wrote a thoroughly sad book about the destruction of a people and their worldview—it is amazing how quickly something so ancient can vanish—that takes as its title a nice little bit from the Book of Isaiah: *Strangers Devour the Land*. Indeed they do. In it a Cree hunter tells him:

> Here is what I think about the bush. The wilderness is just like a store where you can get all of what you need. Everything I needed to survive on came from the land. Of course, I could never part with my land. If somebody lost his land, it would be just like shooting him. All the animals on this land, the moose, the deer, the beaver, the lynx, the fish, all these animals have gone down in the past few years [with the increasing incursions of whites]. I hope this doesn't go too far, for this is the only way we know to survive, this store that is put before us to feed our children from. All this that I've been talking about will be gone soon when it's flooded. When I first heard about this James Bay proposal, I wondered about it for a very long time.

This was in 1972. Apparently others thought the land was like a store, too, not necessarily a homey health-food co-op, but this makes you wonder as well: why do *they* get to have the store they want, and those others do not? In the opening of this store, spiritually akin to The Home Depot, nothing like lives were at stake. What they did not consider was that something even more important was: *the relationship with one's birthplace*. Instead the deal was to provide 30 percent of the electricity Canada had been producing—and sell some of it down south to a somewhat more intemperate neighbor country.

In 1864 George Perkins Marsh published *Man and Nature; or, Physical Geography as Modified by Human Action,* another of those greatly influential books that have not influenced anything much. He had it all down: "Man has too long forgotten that the earth was given to him for usufruct alone, not for consumption, still less for profligate waste." And, "man is everywhere a disturbing agent. Wherever he plants his foot, the harmonies of nature are turned to discords." Even at that early time it was possible to witness, on the more or less blank slate of the American landscape, the stupefying powers of destruction wielded by these mammals who are both astonishingly brilliant and not half smart enough. But he should have seen what was coming.

Around the same time New York City was rubbing its chin in contemplation of turning faraway valleys into pipes to service its water closets, San Francisco was on the other coast doing the same. That city was looking out the corners of its eyes toward the magnificence of Hetch Hetchy, in Yosemite National Park. It was one hundred and fifty miles away, but distance was less a deterrent than, at least one is tempted to think, a motivator to the perverse heart of the human. Starting in 1908 a huge battle was waged in the halls of highest government; from the side of the preservationists, eloquence and incredulity (and five thousand letters) flowed. And you know what those are worth. "Dam Hetch Hetchy! As well dam for water-tanks the people's cathedrals and churches, for no holier temple has ever been consecrated by the heart of man," famously expounded John Muir, the founder of that quaint little group of bird-watchers, the Sierra Club. He knew enough to acknowledge, however, that "sad experience shows that there are people good enough and bad enough for anything." And so there were, with Congress passing the Raker Act in 1913. The dam thus permitted was finished in 1923, and now-unseen beauty lies underwater. We look on such a great work of mankind with awe—and a slight sickness in our guts. *If he can do this to that, what can be done to me?* whispers the trembling subconscious, the one thing that never comes to light.

More than trembling would occur if we were not so privileged to be on the other side of the world from, and therefore basically oblivious to, what the great governments of China and India are up to. The scope of the projects, both proposed and under way, is nothing short of stunning. In fact they are so big the mind shuts down in trying to conceive of them, rather than risk a shower of sparks from the hairline and some nasty gray smoke from the ears. Well over one million people will have been relocated from their homes when the Three Gorges Dam project in China is completed; it will form a reservoir 370 miles long and is the world's biggest hydroelectric project. It will destroy 1,300 archaeological sites, the continuous history of people who are perceived as so many domesticated animals by those who decide. The farmers will, as always, lose the river bottom, the most fertile land there is, and in many cases will be relocated to some inhospitable wasteland that can grow few crops, for reasons not the least of which is lack of water. The purposes of these dams are once again to provide water for rapidly developing urban areas, and to repair the propensity for flooding caused in the first place by wetlands and lakes lost to overdevelopment. The right hand takes while the left hand gives.

Tens of thousands of farmers are protesting the construction of the Pubugou Dam on the Dadu River in southwest China, and the Sichuan government sent in armed troops after they held a sit-in demonstration that lasted almost four days. Some of the elders have been named the "dare-to-dies" since they met the police with shouts of "Kill us! Kill us! Then we won't have to move!"

The Tiger Leaping Gorge project is on hold, but, given past example, its permanent suppression would not be a good bet. When built on the Jinsha River, it will threaten a high gorge that is one of the most dramatic in the world, in the midst of a landscape so biologically diverse it has been designated a UN World Heritage site. And one hundred thousand farmers and herdsmen, the voiceless and marginal, would lose their homes and all that goes with them.

It is almost a secret that many of the grandest projects are planned for seismically vulnerable areas, or risk buildups of silt that could disable the dams with even greater consequences than the great consequences already embraced. *Full steam ahead!* say the blind, welcoming the whistle of the torpedos. India is thinking about making a "Garland of Rivers" that will dwarf even Three Gorges in size. It does not seem altogether promising for the general well-being, given that a prior project, the Tehri Dam on the Bhagirathi River, was built on a fault line. One hundred thousand villagers lost their homes for it, too. Another small factor in the future of these huge river diversions is the waterways' insistence on traversing borders and being melded to ecosystems not just where the dams and weirs are built but along their entire paths and beyond. And so the Ganges and the Brahmaputra, whose waters will be asked to come instead to drought-afflicted areas of India, will not do as they please and sustain the people of Bangladesh, whose misfortune it is to have chosen to be born in a country situated at the end point of so many rivers that pass through India first. The great majority of Bangladesh's twenty million farmers grow rice, but with no water what will become of them? Some prognosticators believe they know what will become of the Sunderbans, which is the world's largest coastal forest. Already, water diversion has caused the mouths of rivers that empty into the Bay of Bengal to start silting up, which is killing the trees, as well as the fish. And so, to another World Heritage site, good-bye.

Then come up with something, if you're so smart. This piece of the puzzle simply does not fit that empty spot; search, and you'll find it does not go in anywhere. Frustration bleeds into madness. The conservative estimate is that four thousand children die every day as a result of drinking contaminated water. Worldwide, one billion people lack access to clean water. Now, the pulling begins: within the next century, there may well be an additional four billion people on earth; but there will be no more water than there is now, and now there is barely enough. We live on 1 percent of the planet's water supply: two thirds of all the fresh water in the world is frozen blue. And those glaciers—here comes another mean yank—are melting.

Let them drink bottled! cries the beautiful queen, as the World Bank renders its verdict that "one way or another, water will soon be moved around the world as oil is now."

While I was busy turning into an adolescent, while I was caring about what color Levi's cords to buy next, while I was sleeping, the temperature was rising. Creeping up so slowly it seemed to have no effect. But accumulating, accumulating. Since the youth of the seventies, more than two degrees Celsius higher, at least in the European Alps, where the melting glaciers have made the summer flow in rivers twice as great. The future was crumbling, while I slept. In Africa, the glaciers will be gone in another twenty years. This is where the Nile originates, and the headwaters of the great river are slowing to a trickle. In a few decades, the people who come up with names will have to get busy, as there will be no more glaciers in Glacier National Park. We melt the ancient ice on which life depends. We are mighty indeed.

There are now so many reservoirs in the northern hemisphere that the planet's center of gravity is forever changed. And so the earth spins imperceptibly faster, because of us.

"BROWN'S STATION, SITUATED on the line of the Ulster & Delaware Railroad is the first village in Olive that we come to after leaving Ashton in Hurley. It is a quiet little spot with stores, postoffice, telegraph service, schools and churches, and attracts a large number of summer boarders each year. The Beaverkill flows through this end of the township . . . and offers many an attractive spot and pretty nook along its winding way for the loiterings of the city worn sojourners who are seeking rest here during the summer months." So writes "the Artist," name of R. Lionel DeLisser, who beginning in 1896 authored an eight-part series on "Picturesque Ulster" that was meant to appeal to the many who escaped the heat of New York City by spending summer weeks in the dozens of boardinghouses that salted the county's countryside. There were ample streams for fishing and rocky forest rambles for visitors in the slowness of days under the shadow of the Catskill Mountains. Outside of the busy port of the Rondout and the ferry across the Hudson, in nearby Kingston, the business of the county's hamlets varied from bluestone quarrying and milling to small farming, taking in those summer boarders, and realizing the little self-sufficiencies of turn-of-the-century America, which were essentially the same as those at the turn of the previous century, too.

It was not even noticed for a while, because the people were not the suspicious sort, that some men previously unknown in the region were going around taking test borings. Their work was highly serious; to prove it, their drills were tipped with black diamonds—each of which "was valued at about $100, making the diamonds alone worth $700 in each drill," marveled a contemporary account. And even if these strange doings had been noticed, it could hardly have been understood what the final outcome of such arcane inspections might be. But now it is possible to see the building of this unprecedented dam as a sort of dust-to-dust parable, since the place they chose as ideal for a reservoir of Esopus waters was the site of a former, prehistoric lake. Man would simply refill it.

It is just like us to never agree on the meaning of the Indian names we retain—how badly mangled we'll never know—on our maps of stolen places. "Ashokan" may or may not mean "place of many fishes" in some aboriginal tongue. Still, it is what we cling to, and it is certainly appropriate, only more so with the place covered in water up to 150 feet deep and, no longer dependent on the vagaries of nature, carefully stocked with sport fish by the Department of Environmental Conservation. Then again, it may mean "crossing the creek." Or maybe "blackbird."

Being hit with eminent domain is a bit like being jumped in a dark street late at night: one minute you're walking along, and the next you've got someone's arm tight against your throat. Your legs tilt at nothing but air. That futile kicking of the two thousand people who were summarily ordered to leave their homes and farms, stores and depots and churches—within ten days of filing the map with the county clerk and paying one half the assessed valuation of a property, the city might legally seize it, bam—took place in small local courtrooms. But there was really no stopping what was going to happen.

By most current accounts, to the people of the Esopus Valley who were to be displaced, the scent of money was more powerful than the smell of smoke from their burning houses. It is said they quickly calmed down when they saw how much money the big city was willing to lavish on lawyers, and they thought to get themselves some of that, too. But does this accord with what you know of things? It is just that it happened so many years ago. The people are long dead now. Their children recall something, but they're not entirely sure what.

The people involved in this slow-motion struggle, back and forth, between the takers and the taken might as well be out of a medieval allegory: a lawyer who fought vociferously for the people against the city was named Clearwater; a woman who made a claim for $7,665 in damages on her property—those drillers and surveyors had left behind a broken fence through which her cow escaped, and she wanted $50 for the animal and $144.28 for the milk thus lost—was named Flood. The whole legal epic concluded some twenty-five years on.

It is not until you look at what happened later, in the mirror of the further condemnation of people's farms and small towns deeper into the Catskills, that you see the emotions are simply fresher there. Rawer. The anger still lingers around the Ashokan, too; that is how you know it could not quite be as the books say. It is anger translated, true, like the children's game telephone, in which a phrase is whispered into one ear and on and on down the line, until what emerges from the last child's mouth is eroded, or polished, like sea glass.

THEY CAME IN like occupying troops, and foreign ones at that. The people who had been there were outnumbered by the new ones who came, by two to one. The new ones were different, all right, having been brought straight from Ellis Island, where they had learned to be grateful for work, or the sharecroppers' shacks of Georgia, where they had learned to handle mules. They were put up (the "colored" separately, of course, according to the lousy dictates of the time) in a new bustling town that rose from the bare dirt over the grave of poor old Brown's Station. Now it became a not-so-quiet little spot, with brand-new "stores, postoffice, . . . schools and churches," in addition to two hundred multiroom houses, seven dorms, nineteen barracks, bakery, barbershop, hospital, kitchen, ice house, commissary, bank, firehouse, and other necessary establishments that suddenly sprouted there. The barns for the horses of the police force—larger than any seen or required by the previous settlements near the spot—were made of wood salvaged from other barns torn down in advance of the coming water.

What these workers built on top of what they destroyed over the years from 1907 to 1914 inspires amazement. The Catskill Aqueduct that was built prior to it, to get the water from this ten-thousand-acre lake of fresh water to the people who demanded it, is even more astounding.

This is an occasion for unreserved pride in American genius which has achieved a stupendous engineering triumph. Starting at an elevation of 610 feet above tide level in the Catskill mountains, and creating four large lakes on its way, the aqueduct burrows under valleys, tunnels through mountains, dives under rivers to a depth of 1,114 feet below sea-level, bores through the solid rock of Manhattan Island, and delivers pure mountain water to every borough of the city. It is 120 miles long and is capable of delivering 500,000,000 gallons of water a day. The greatest of the famous Roman aqueducts was only half as long as this one,

wrote Edward H. Hall in 1917 in his three-hundred-year history of New York City's water woes and wonders. An excerpt of the book was reprinted a few years ago by a local press that saw fit to temper the worship of this feat—the commemorative medal made at its completion by the Catskill Aqueduct Celebration Committee crowned it nothing less than "An Achievement of Civic Spirit, Scientific Genius and Faithful Labor"—with a prologue voicing a slight dissent: "Today we can be sure that whether it is the people of New York City who pay, or the people living within the Catskill Mountain watershed who are forced to pay for a resource they cannot use, the results will be the same. . . . New York City will have the pure water it needs to continue to grow." Indeed, Hall's entire history is many gallons that can be boiled down to a few ounces: growth, commonly called progress, is the gurgling spring from which displacement flows.

THERE WERE 954 individual parcels in 11 hamlets; the earliest property dated back to 1740. And there were some 2,800 bodies, or what remained of them, from 32 cemeteries—most of these were removed by the relatives who could be found, who received fifteen dollars apiece for their trouble, with an additional three to deal with the headstone—so let it not be said the city was uninterested in history. With the bodies all gone, the final digging up of the past could commence. All brush, all trees, all stumps larger than six inches across. All houses, barns, stores, outbuildings; a few were dragged away to continue their lives elsewhere, but the rest were dismantled or torched where they stood. All day, all night, the fires burned and burned, until the coals turned gray with ash. But they remained hot underneath, the heart of the fire. In 1913 a local columnist wrote of West Shokan in her final dispatches from the zone, "The trees are all cut down and the village fading as a dream."

Yet people would remember, forever, because they could do nothing else. Hobart Rowe, who lived in West Hurley in the house built by his father until it was swept away, spent twenty years of his later life in what some might see as a peculiar act of recovery. He rebuilt the village. There, in a scale model, are fifty-four buildings he called forth in all their situational detail from his memory. In a video tour of it, he can explain his motive haltingly, and only so far: "I remembered the families. . . . That was the reason I built." Indeed, he remembered: the names of all the people, all their progeny, their occupations; shops and their wares, barns, topographical elements, sheds, streets, churches, smithies, school, post office, mill, quarry. At eye level, one enters a dollhouse world of small-village life, its wagon road and gentle contours, wood-frame houses, stone walls—everything except the people, who need not be remade from matchsticks and model glue.

What could cause such devotion to a disappeared past? Ask the doctor. In a tale called "The Landscape of His Dreams," Oliver Sacks explains, "Discontinuity and nostalgia are most profound if, in growing up, we leave or lose the place where we were born and spent our childhood, if we become expatriates or exiles, if the place, or the life, we were brought up in is changed beyond recognition or destroyed."

All writing, which comes from the seat of recollection and is always about the writer's past even if it is set in a fictional present, is triggered by a destruction. You are welcome to test this ridiculously generalized theory. *Walking Through Yesterday in Old West*

Hurley is Frank Lee Du Mond's more direct response, written in 1988 about one of the towns that were moved beyond the reach of the reservoir because "he clearly remembered his childhood in the small village which disappeared underwater and could never be visited again." Writers create a place in words in order to revisit a lost home. And sometimes they revisit it for real, too.

> Hunt's Pond was our favorite swimming place. . . . Schoolmate and lifelong friend Elmer (Pat) Johnston photographed me as a stripling basking on the rockpile, a cherished reminder of good times at the old swimming hole. . . . Hunt's Pond is still hidden in its bluestone setting at the north end of the West Hurley dike of the Ashokan Reservoir in the new village. Pat and I met there for several summers in the 1960's and swam together again. Then Pat died of a heart attack one summer at a bank in Kingston. The urge was still so strong to go back to the swimming hole of my youth at Hunt's Pond that I returned alone for several years.

He relates the story of a man for whom such loss was too painful. Eighty-three-year-old Joseph McElvey, former blacksmith, vowed he would never give up his home. In April 1908 he had supper and then left his house with his revolver. For three days they looked for him, the story goes. A clairvoyant was consulted, and she said that Joe would be found near a high ledge. And so it was that he was found on a rock shelf with his loaded pistol beside him. He had died of exhaustion and exposure.

In the epilogue to the book, these words appear: "Frank L. Du Mond remembered the time he actually went home again—a year when the water was so low in the reservoir that he could walk down the mainstreet of the vanished town. He found the large bluestone slab that had held up the family porch. As he stood on it and looked around at the mountains, he was surprised. The view had not changed. It had not really been lost at all."

AERIAL VIEWS OF the reservoir from the storied drought of 1985 show the ghost impressions of life: foundations, roads, rail beds, stone walls. They look like those pictures of the Martian planetscape that people use as evidence that there was once life in a lifeless place.

Where did the water come from? I mean, in the beginning? (That which made us possible.) It began in "gentle cosmic rain," as the physicist said, possibly unaware he is a poet of astonishing powers. It was flung off the surface of icy asteroids streaking past. It would freeze again, and move slowly, a lumbering giver of life, somewhere way down the road. It melted and sunk deep into the land, waiting for us to find it, draw it upward to our uses. This is what we sometimes drink: "fossil water," deposited ten thousand years ago. Maybe water just inspires poetry from all its worldly explicators.

Geographer Yi-Fu Tuan offers (again, again!) in *Topophilia*: "Water is an image of the unconscious. . . . Immersion in water means the extinction of fire and of consciousness. It means death. . . . [T]he emotion associated with water in the Chinese system is fear."

THEY NEEDED MORE. As soon as the Ashokan was finished, they went farther. The Schoharie Creek actually flowed north, but this was as nothing to the remarkable engineers in service to the Board of Water Supply. They could turn this creek so that it would flow south to its new master. The town of Gilboa, previously not for sale, was bought by New York City.

"Inside the take line" is the way they describe the shape of what is to come. Within, everything is taken. In Gilboa, that amounted to 25 houses, 12 barns, a church, a garage, and the final resting places of 1,330 souls. On December 4, 1925, the last boards of a Gilboa farm went spiraling to the sky as smoke. And that was that.

A romantic pen in 1931 inscribed the fate of this newly vanished place:

> For the people who dwelt along the ancient creek, destiny has been . . . unkind. Deprived of their stream of water that tumbles down from the mountains, their fate is like that invoked by David for the mountains of Biblical Gilboa on which both Saul and Jonathan had perished:
>
> *Ye mountains of Gilboa, let there be no dew or rain*
> *upon you,*
> *Neither fields of offerings.*

Now the Shandaken Tunnel brings the Gilboan water eighteen miles under mountains to the Esopus, where it mingles (not always successfully, some say, being highly turbid) with the flow that fills the Ashokan. Another reservoir was built.

Thus spoke Seneca: "Where a spring rises or a river flows, there should we build altars, and offer sacrifices."

THEY WOULD COME HOME and find them nailed to a tree or the side of a building. They were cloth, so that no one could say they didn't see them, that the rain had washed them away. Their meaning was both mystifying—"New York Supreme Court / Sixth Judicial District / Notice of Application for the appointment of commissioners of appraisal / Motion to be made in the . . ."—and altogether too clear. The people had been hearing about this for decades now, so that they didn't really believe it, or didn't really want to believe it, and so didn't, but they could never be truly prepared for the sight of those muslin cloths on something that belonged to them.

The surveyors had been abroad in the countryside again, now to find this place. The water was soft. They would put a dam on the East Branch of the Delaware River just above the village of Downsville. The reservoir would take the name of the first town to be drowned, Pepacton. It was decided in 1938. The water did not begin to collect and rise behind the dam until 1954. So this gave the people a few years to get used to the idea, or a few years in which to never become used to it, a few years in which to grow sad and angry and disbelieving. They would get to stay around and watch their history and the material of their personal lives torn down, ripped apart, and finally burned and drowned. Arena. Pepacton. Shavertown. Union Grove.

When they realized they could do nothing else, some people started leaving; the decline was steady between 1947 and 1955. But they did not go far. Most moved to nearby towns like Andes or Margaretville. A few possessing a peculiar kind of courage climbed the rocky hills on either side of the valley so they could live looking down on where they had been, though for most of these a return to farming was out of the question. At the upper end of the reservoir, they held on as long as they could. For those who stayed, Mary Jackson Shaver remarked many years later, "It became a depressed place. People weren't working on their farms anymore in order to leave them to their children," they were just working them because farms had to be worked, and because they were still there. At last, the houses of Arena were put up for auction in August 1954; most of them sold for between $200 and $400. Barns and outbuildings went for as low as $15. One especially fine house got carted away to a part of the nearby hamlet of Dunraven that wasn't taken by the city as buffer for the reservoir.

After they had been sold to the city when the condemnation process was begun, many houses remained the homes of the folks who had always lived in them. Only now they had to pay rent to the City of New York. "It is interesting to notice the difference in the way the payments must be made when it's you who owes the city," wrote one woman in an article detailing the legal labyrinths in which she wandered for months and years while waiting for full payment after the city took possession of her farm. Many of the dispossessed took jobs on the reservoir project, which might be compared to something like those unforgettable historical acts in which victims have been forced to dig their own graves, except that this time they were paid $1.90 per hour to do it, which was decent money for these former farmers.

Sometime in the late 1870s, the famous naturalist and writer John Burroughs built his own small boat—this a thing that a man of that time was able to do with just enough thought and discipline, and not as today only with a pile of money and tools from Lowe's and a Rodale plan book and very smelly glue and a heated garage—with the intention of floating in it down the East Branch. "In its watershed I was born and passed my youth, and here on its banks my kindred sleep," he says in the preface of a book he titled after its first essay, "Pepacton." He goes on to describe the wild beauty of the mountains through which the river cut, and then an anecdote: "About half a century ago a pious Scotch family, just arrived in this country, came through this gorge. One of the little boys, gazing upon the terrible desolation of the scene, so unlike in its savage and inhuman aspects anything he had ever seen at home, nestled close to his mother, and asked with bated breath, 'Mither, is there a God here?'"

No matter what the answer was to that question, there were increasing numbers of white settlers, the first of whom had arrived around 1770 to encounter and later fight with indigenous people. Indian relics were being plowed up by farmers into the 1940s. Now we are fairly certain that "pepacton" means "marriage of the waters," even though someone else went and wrote that it in fact means "calamus or sweet flag place." (Maybe this was the Indians' way of saying we never would fully own their land.) Then in 1781 Jacob and John Shaver came to the place that would be named for them. What they saw there could well have been God, but it was also trees: forests of huge trees, among them great hemlocks, which gave rise to the area's first industry. Arena was originally called Lumberville. They cut the trees and then lashed them together in rafts, and when the spring freshets raised the river and made it fast they went riding down the swift current to Philadelphia. It was not an entirely sane thing to do.

When the trees were largely gone, there was rocky land up the hillsides. Some of the bottomland was good for growing, but one thing this land excelled at was making cows happy. In 1893 Will Close of Arena won first prize for butter at the Chicago World's Fair. And butter was a big deal. When the city finished taking their 13,384 acres, they took with them 82 dairy farms, on which 1,856 cows had grazed on the mineral-rich grass. That also meant the closure of local creameries, which even if not inside the take line, no longer had a long queue of farmers ponying up their many silver milk cans every day. In *History and Stories of Margaretville and Surrounding Area*, Ethel H. Bussy reports, "Delaware County lost its preeminent place in the list of top milk-producing counties in the State when [the] Pepacton Reservoir was built," a terse update of a prereservoir history that remarked, "As Dairying always has been the principal industry in Delaware County, it undoubtedly always will be, because of the climate, soil and topography of the area."

This land had also kept the summer boarders well fed. "In these hills of glory lies a little valley, parted by a stream silver in the sunshine, flowing just enough to play a melody that once heard is never forgotten.... We ... hope to meet the best approval with our produce." If that advertisement for a boardinghouse seems to entice with prose tinged purple, not to mention a perfect little dying fall, know that in fact it was painted after the true hues of life here in the East Branch. It was an enchanted place. All the people who lived here say so.

There was no great wealth, but there was no poverty either. It was just a place where everyone not only knew everyone else but felt deep inside that they were all essentially one big family. What was rich was life itself, the days in an environment that would seem to issue its stern warnings against human habitation with great regularity: in the Catskill Mountains it is said there are three seasons, winter, summer, and mud. There is no month, except perhaps July, in which snow has not been recorded. The water in April and May boils down from the hills and enters the valleys with a roaring that fills the ears. The winter stream sometimes breaks its ice for sport, taking the bridges and any unhappy crossers along with them. The work is hard, as any farmer's work in pre-agribusiness days is hard, but the entertainments are recompense. Baseball is all-absorbing. So are the horse races at the fair. There are silent movies for a nickel, and sometimes dancing, and always church suppers. Everyone goes to the swimming hole in summer, and when the snow comes there is sledding, sleighing, ice fishing. The kids learn every rock and puddle and woodlot in the region by the time they are ten. Mary Belle Nohejl, who lived in Shavertown from the time she was six, said later that the whole township of Andes was "like a big playground." She and her friends went blueberry picking, sometimes finding the best fruit in the cemetery, which did not please her mother. Underneath the big iron bridge that crossed the river at Shavertown was a sort of lover's lane.

Dorothy McCune Andrews was born in Shavertown in 1919, in a house that only the previous day had received electricity. Thus was the place portrayed in another boardinghouse ad: "Shavertown is a lively country village with three churches, Presbyterian, Advent and Catholic, three stores, two barber shops, some 75 residences and many advantages." Although one wanting a little more excitement could go over to Arena and join the Pistol Club at Stan's Tavern—"drink 'till twelve and pistol two." On the Andrews farm was the site of the illustrious Shavertown Fair. In 1897 it attracted an estimated 2,500 to 4,000 people, "which is certainly a large crowd when we consider that all must come from a distance and in wagons," said the paper. Mrs. Andrews tells of a way of life that is hard to imagine now, so imagine it: youngsters "weren't entertained, we entertained ourselves." Of course, as did all farm children, she worked from an early age and did not have many toys, although she fondly recalls a teeter-totter. When the chores were done, her parents might play cards; her mother would get an apple from the barrel downstairs. Then they would listen to *Amos 'n' Andy* on the radio. Everyone went to church, naturally. And the rhythm of life and work would be happily interrupted by maple-sugaring parties, ice-cream making, dances in Fletcher's Hall or the rented Grange. There were two or three mails a day, brought in on the Delaware & Eastern railroad, as was the great quantity of feed required in an ecomony based on the labors of domesticated animals.

Then the surveyors came at last. There had been talk of it for years. But now you could find the ugly reality of stakes in the ground, taunting. When he came upon them, Dorothy's father would pull them up, heave them into the air with a strength born of anger and fear. When the condemnation flags started appearing, she says, "It was pretty sad. And even then, I don't think they realized what was going to happen, until they saw it happen." She remembers people seeming stunned, wondering where they were going to move and how they were going to make a living. Some people got together at Fletcher's Hall to voice their opposition, but where were the ears to hear it? Nothing previously experienced by the small-town folk could have led them to know what to do about this. It would only amount to futile kicking. Although for years many would, of course, wonder if there wasn't *something* they could have dreamed up to do. In a 1954 article in the *Courier Magazine* ("The Human Interest Publication of the Southern Tier and Central New York State") titled "Ghost Town Along the Delaware," the wishful power of hindsight is evident. George Youmans, native of Shavertown, wondered aloud,

> Maybe if, when those surveyors and such came through here 20 years ago, the people had taken up their guns and chased them off the land, claiming that their constitu-

tional rights were violated . . . maybe then we wouldn't be where we are now. But that was long ago. . . . Lord, I was only 18 when they first came through here with their telescopes and lines and such. I guess folks around here should have known right then that their time in Shavertown was limited.

But of course it was: Shavertown was, to its inhabitants, very nearly paradise. The hills embraced it in soft arms as would a mother. Apart from its physical beauty, it embodied qualities so ineffable that to blow on them would disperse them forever, like milkweed in a breeze. It contained the whole of American history, that's all: it was as alive and ever-flowing as the cold, clear waters of the East Branch. The things they did here, and they way they did them, were fundamentally unchanged from those of the first Dutchmen who made their tentative explorations here nearly two hundred years before, notwithstanding the coming of the train and then the automobile and the occasional tractor. What they did in expunging this place and filling it with water was as if you did the same to a fine museum with its interpretive exhibits and irreplaceable artifacts. Five nineteenth-century schoolhouses that used to reside in the Town of Colchester are now underwater.

The *Catskill Mountain News* described the constant sound of dynamite as "a roar like that of giant ashcans tumbling down the mountainsides." It also wanted its readers to know that "beyond the blueprints of the engineers, behind the smoke of the dynamite blasts ripping out granite, lie a thousand small tragedies." Local papers in fact excelled at getting the tone of anguish just right: "This Valley Is DOOMED" headlined one; another described the area's future as "a midcentury Atlantis peopled only by fish."

At the historical society the pictorial evidence of small tragedies, in black and white, is drily captioned and calls only for turning of the plastic sleeves. "Tearing down Union Grove." "Pushing over Chimney of Miller House." In sequence, until only the foundation is left. A plume of black smoke is seen rising high above the valley, as if it needs to go somewhere to tell someone. The pictures make it look like a race to erase the village: the dam is filling up, and still the rubbish burns by the side of farmhouses and barns. Soon, even the birds are gone. The workers on the project made sure nothing was left, hunting down everything on ground or in sky for food.

At the auctions, neighbors bought neighbors' belongings. There was no compensation paid for moving expenses or the real costs of relocation.

Evelyn Norris, who was born in Union Grove in 1940, says her grandparents watched their house be torn down. As she relates it, fifty years later, she cries. Some people could not be made to go near the site of destruction of their own places; others could not stay away. The house was hooked by a corner and pulled over, then bulldozed into a pile and doused with gasoline. As they watched it burn, the grandfather said to his wife, "Well, Deb, there goes our whole life. We have nothing left now." Mrs. Inez Atkins, resident of Shavertown and its postmistress for thirty years, told *The New York Times* in 1949, "The city has no sentiment. This has been my home for thirty-seven years. I have friends and know my community. When they transplant me it will be difficult. There's no room for newcomers, especially old folks, in a new community." What she puts her finger on here is an odd paradox: the closeness, the helpfulness, the kindly beneficence of these small towns toward members of their own—and their coldness toward, unwillingness to welcome in, anyone who does not already belong. But let us quickly leave this rude interruption in our contemplation of heaven on earth. One farmer, with a six-hundred-acre farm near Downsville that was considered one of the prettiest around, sold reasonably willingly to the city in the first negotiations for thirty thousand dollars, which he thought quite fair. Still, he said, "as quitting time gets closer the thought of leaving my home, the buildings I built and the place I raised my family makes me sick."

But what really shook the people was the cemeteries; we

remain strangely attached to our dead. Yet the Board of Water Supply directives seemed positively unmoved: REMOVAL OF BODIES, they trumpeted in huge type. "Upon the satisfactory removal of said remains and the said monuments and other distinguishing marks . . . the following allowances to be paid . . . : For the removal of the remains, refilling the grave, purchase of new lot and reinterment in a new grave $65.00 per grave." Perhaps what disturbed people most was the thought of having to break a sort of covenant: that body was put into that earth to rest forever, so they could be dust to dust. That's why they went with shovels themselves whenever they could. They were afraid the bones would get mixed up, and somehow the re-placed stone that says great-grandfather rested below would be made to lie. Sometimes the dead were nowhere to be found. The fine dirt was sifted and all that was found was a brooch, a tie clasp, a few coffin nails. In their own way, the departed thus insisted on staying where they were. The bones were long intermixed anyway: the Shavertown cemetery had been situated on the site of an Indian burying ground.

There was little left to do except wrangle over money. The city convened a commission of appraisal, before which property holders could bring their cases, consisting of three arbiters: one from the county affected, one from the city, and one from elsewhere in New York State. Then the lawyers got busy, as lawyers are wont to do. The testimony, on everything from house paint to the types of fish that could survive in the altered temperatures of the released water below the dam, is a textbook on the legal arts, albeit one extending to 399 volumes—and that is only for a portion of the fifty-seven years covering Delaware County cases. The rest, if saved, await discovery in municipal archives and in whatever sad graves useless old office files get buried. This board was finally dissolved in 1994, although it could be reconvened if someone arose with a new complaint; the dead were requested to stay underground. While they met, the City of New York Delaware Water Supply Commissioners of Appraisal settled 6,700 claims totaling $28,806,168.

As the water began rising behind the Downsville dam in 1954, there were a few pieces of unfinished business left. One was to dismantle the iron bridge at Shavertown, the one that appears, in all its quaint and geometric handsomeness, in just about every photograph taken of the old town since photographers roved the countryside taking postcard views that were to be inscribed with handwritten legends. But the bridge would not be taken. Suddenly it crumpled, to fall into the water where it was left. Sometimes now it, too, rises from the ghosty deeps. Not so another bridge that had to go, remembered Union Grove's Evelyn Norris: "When the iron bridge came down it was scary—my first thought was, Lord, how are we going to get to Arena?" Such is the persistence of habit, or desire; but there would be no Arena to get to.

Fletcher's Hall, once a creamery and later a place of community amusement, was the scene of Shavertown's farewell party on New Year's Eve. As the new year was born, the old town died an unnatural death.

At the last page, the book shuts on the places that used to be home on the East Branch of the Delaware. It is over. Yet another almost immediately opens, fresh and unwritten, near the waters of the West Branch twenty miles away. Or is it in fact a different story? Everything feels as if we have read it before: the big Delaware County creameries, standing proud by the river, ready to receive the riches of the Holsteins. The small villages in which there was no crime to speak of, because it would be like transgressing against your own kin. Instead, these were places where people did such things as volunteer to get laid off at the creamery during a bad time so that another fellow with young children could keep his job, or tell the deliveryman where the box of money was under the counter at the barbershop and just to take what he required. These took place so recently it could have been in your very own childhood. But they also occurred in a world that is so far off you couldn't find a remnant of it anymore. Cannonsville. Granton. Beerston. Rock Royal. Rock Rift.

In Cannonsville, which was called "a place where something

was always happening" by one of its happy residents, Lor-Gene's restaurant was one of the spots where those things happened: it served ice cream to crowds of summer campers and hamburgers to people who drove all the way from Binghamton to get them. It had only recently been transformed (through painstaking hand-work by its new owners, Gene and Lorraine Weixlbaum) from its former situation as drugstore as well as pool hall and barbershop when the condemnation flag was nailed to it. Gene tore it off. Another was put up. Gene tore it off. They had to threaten him with jail to get him to quit. They didn't care about the depths of his frustration: it positively went against nature to condemn a perfectly good building.

The condemnation flags started appearing in 1955. Groundbreaking had already taken place on the West Delaware tunnel, another marvel, which would bring the water 44 miles closer to the city that desired it. The "taking date" for property spanned 1955 to 1963; what was taken would comprise 19,910 acres, or 31.1 square miles. Soon every building was painted with large red numbers—one hesitates to call them scarlet—to direct the grubbing contractor. Nine hundred and forty-one people, of whom 405 were children, had to move. Gone forever would be 68 dairy farms and their 2,138 cows, two creameries, 26 farms of other types, four cemeteries, and seven burying grounds.

Anticipating this loss, the people of the West Branch tried to get New York City to consider filtering water from the Hudson River instead, a source that had been proposed many times previous and was long before rejected as "virtually a reservoir of infection." Now, in 1951, a report to the mayor sniffed that New York City residents "are accustomed to and they are entitled to be served by the much superior upland waters." In March 1955, the Board of Water Supply met and took approximately three minutes to appropriate $85 million for the first phase that would lead to the Cannonsville reservoir. Their vote was unopposed.

The city was seen as high-handed and even as gratuitously cruel. One farmer, it was reported, saw the ripe apples in an orchard newly acquired by the city going unharvested, a deeply offensive sight to anyone raised on the land. After he had picked his lot, BWS police appeared and ordered him to dump them back onto the ground to rot.

Only a witness farther removed from the scene than those who were there to weep quietly on the day their houses were put aflame could see as a paramount loss the architectural wonder of an immense stone dairy barn built in 1899. In pictures it looks at once Dutch, ancient with moss, and Constructivist. The city had to work extra hard to blow it up. Or the 160-year-old homestead of Benjamin Cannon, so grand that horses would haul directly into the basement the six-foot logs consumed by some of its many fireplaces. Or his son's gracious house, called Chestnut Point and lately inhabited by the Judd family. A niece who had lived there described what it was like when she went to see it for the last time: "There was not one of the big, beautiful trees standing. The only thing left was the house, and it looked so desolate, like looking at something in a desert. I had to pull my car over to the side of the road, because I was crying so hard."

The emotion that underlay the tears was soon to encompass even more than these immediate excisions; time after time, perhaps only years later, people realized they mourned most their inability to show their children where they had come from. For some reason, this felt worse than the losses of the places themselves. It was as if some part of the leg itself had disappeared, and the urge to walk again was continuous and permanently thwarted.

Benjamin Cannon had also erected, in 1809, the type of building no town of that era that believed adamantly in its future would lack: a stately three-story hotel that presents a bold public face of colonnaded porches across its front. On July 4, 1956, a gigantic American flag was unfurled from it for the last Cannonsville Old Home Day. Thousands came, to gather and eat and reminisce over what was not yet quite gone. The highlight of the day was a parade that presented the town's history in the form of floats and costumed marchers: it began with "Indians" (an island in the West Branch had been an important council ground of the Delawares) and continued with a float devoted to the Merry Delvers Literary Society of Cannonsville, a club active since its founding in 1889 and dedicated to "merrily delving into literature." Another float presented a tableau of the seasons of the farming life. Finally came a group of boys hoisting papier-mâché fishes—the end of the line for Cannonsville. The program for the event rapidly sold out its entire press run of one thousand copies. The History Committee, composed of Mrs. Leland B. Boyd, Miss Antoinette K. Owens, and Mr. and Mrs. George E. Judd, captured the entire arc of their town's passage in two formidable sentences.

> One hundred eighty years ago this was a wilderness which belonged to the bear, the panther, the wolf, and the Indian. Now it is our turn to be bought off for a few strings of wampum while our homes and land sink under a man-made sea to be inhabited by fishes which will take refuge under rocks etched by the fossil remains of their still more ancient ancestors.

THE CITIZENS WERE able to fire back, in a way. The water in the Cannonsville Reservoir ended up being pretty bad, due to a high level of phosphates that may be the legacy of more than a century of excretions in the soil from all those cows. The impounded water is primarily used to regulate the flow of the Delaware River to levels decreed by the U.S. Supreme Court in 1954. But the revenge is hardly sweet. It is now considered "the reservoir that didn't have to be," as the title of a recent angry two-part history of the project by Dorothy Kubik in *Kaatskill Life* put it. In a letter to the magazine, the city was compared to terrorists: "Like our World Trade Center, Rock Royal was here and then it was gone. And all a heart-rending waste that need not have happened." But it did.

THERE IS A KIND of thermostat in the human soul that clicks on when the emotional mercury rises all the way to the top and finds nowhere higher to go. It signals the production of poetry.

An unnamed resident of Shavertown published a prayer for the lost town:

> As we later ride along that highway
> And anxiously look down
> We'll hold a picture in our hearts
> Of home, and Shavertown.
>
> If all the tears we shed like rain,
> Could heal the wounds thou hast,
> After all the pain you suffered
> May God grant you peace at last.

A compatriot had a sharper pencil.

> Now the axe of condemnation
> Has fallen on your head
> Your people all have scattered
> With a listless, weary tread
> To find a place to live in
> Which never will be home,
> Like travelers now in exile
> Cast on the world to roam.
> Man's home was once his castle,
> He's seen it torn to shreds;
> The hallowed place where once it stood
> Will be the river's bed.

A battered, plundered, smoking ruin,
Oh for eyes that cannot see
Or ears that cannot hear
Or feel, this endless misery.
Other little towns we know,
Their fate will be the same,
This monster creeping to consume
Power of Eminent Domain.
Our cry for help proved useless
Oh what could stay this cruel hand!
We, the victims and the vanquished
Yield to the will of man.

Steve Pelletier was moved to write "Cannonsville," which ends:

They moved our forebears, too,
and twice buried they rest today in drier graves.
But their souls, with ours, pass aqueous days
looking up at the anglers who, stopping,
drop long baited lines to tease
fish that with our diluted dreams
weave amidst waterlogged beams
and rotted frames.
On watery summer walks we think
what fun if once they snared not perch or bass
but a soggy memento—a soaked Bible or sampler
or a sodden old dress. Or, better, a native,
who could tell them about the fishing
and the history drowned there.

And Dorothy Kubik's voice could not satisfy itself in the prose of her history of Cannonsville and its travails alone; it would take verse for full expression. Part 2 of "On Pepacton Reservoir" begins:

He has not let go,
Not yet,
Even though the cows have been sold,
And house and barn and saphouse and sheds
Stripped, ready for the bulldozer.
He clings to one last mark—
That hemlock on the hillside
At the corner of their land.
Lost in the anonymity of forest,
It will survive this wrenching:
His one last hold
On this portion of earth
That had defined him to himself.

The tone and substance of Janet Hartmann's poem "To the Invaders" is adequately conveyed by its title. But it is too bad you can't see the creative anger that led to another variety of art, as only you could if you stood before John Hopkins's large painting of the Pepacton that is at the Andes Society for History and Culture. The Catskills rise like a quilt of colors at the top, while at the bottom the painter has recourse to prose: "Jan. 1988 some 400 claims unresolved; when and if resolved settlement will be in 1950–1956 dollars. NO INTEREST NO INFLATION ADJUSTMENTS." In large red letters below this is painted his final word: "Where there is no truth in actions, there is no trust, no belief in equitable Solutions." But what stays with you, perhaps longer than you might like, is the central image. There are all the villages again, their trees and fields and farmhouses, but now a blue scrim of water floats over them. Still there, and gone. It is just what has haunted you for a long time.

THE AIR IS DIFFERENT in the Catskills; it has an added dimension. The vistas do, too, and cause you to adjust your vision to take in what seems impossible: the sweep, the distances, a feeling that you have been lifted out of time and placed where all around you is earth still in its infancy. This closeness to the past has served to shelter the communities of man so that they seem little altered by the overturning changes that have remade everyplace else. I once had a home in the Catskills. The desire to live and sleep and walk the land there again is so overpowering it is eerie. I am regularly visited by a spirit of something dead to me.

In his grand history, *The Catskills*, Alf Evers said, "Mountains everywhere are likely to become conservative places to which change comes slowly and where the past clings desperately to life and where people, especially older people like those in whom the Catskills abound, cling for comfort to the past." Their communities are insular. They have to rely on themselves and one another. Much of life consists of moving rock; the type of soil is aptly described by the title of a recent history of Delaware county: *Two Stones for Every Dirt*. The weather wants to kill you there. It is where I first heard in the night the haunting cries of eastern coyotes, which some naturalists believe are actually part wolf, and what they were crying was that this was really theirs. I believed them. This has always been a place where the solitary feel at home.

> The lonely huts [of the hoop shavers] on these mountain-sides fulfilled a real need of the Eastern part of this country, which possesses no deserts. For it was always into the desert that the hermit would flee to find peace for his soul. Throughout all the centuries of history the desert was the place to which the ascetic looked to escape from the conventions of his fellows. There he could waste his time. From time immemorial, too, men have known that the solitude, the vast unbroken levels, of the desert perpetually turned a man's thoughts inward. The solitude and silence "lead men out in vaguest reverie," or "make one prone to aimless dreams."

The vocation referred to above by H. A. Haring, in his 1931 book *Our Catskill Mountains*, is the making of wooden barrel hoops, a fine occupation for those who like to work alone. The industry flourished in the mountains between 1880 and 1890, then collapsed due to the invention of a machine for cutting hoops.

Until quite recently there remained other jobs in these mountains for hermits. Almost any job is, in fact. Finding ways to stay warm in a drafty farmhouse. The dogs' daily constitutional, up the rocky steepness just in back of the house, through woods that a hundred years ago were no longer woods, with stone walls now tumbling backward in their own history, and past remnants of a farm so far gone they might be chimeras: is this a drinking cistern for livestock, handily made to collect water from a vanished spring—or is it just an odd happenstance of rocks around a sinkhole that is always slightly damp? Going to work in a distant township on cold gray afternoons, an hour's drive during which you pass *not a single person*. You think, not entirely unhappy, that maybe you are the last one on earth.

Much of the drive goes by the edge of a long lake that mirrors the clouds within a fringe of pine. By now you have come to instinctively recoil from this passage in the trip, driving faster than you ought to on the curving road. It's as if something has suddenly changed; this is not normal Catskills loneliness here. There is something dark and heavy. It almost makes you afraid. The scene looks, once more, the way it might have to the first white people to gaze upon it: bereft of any life but that of the fearsome beast. *Is there a God here?*

One day, after you learn the story, it becomes clear. The lake breathes something into the air. It is sadness. The air around this water is full of sadness.

THE MOUNTAINOUS REGION is undergoing its transformation. The place to which, in its native conservativeness, change is slow to come has been forced to welcome it. The final remnant of the Way It

Used to Be is on the way out, and this is how you know the end is near: when not everyone waves to everyone else. Five years ago they still did. But I have been witness to its vanishing in neighboring Ulster County—which acts much as the canary in the coal mine for Delaware County—and over the past couple of years the number of folks here who wave as they drive past has dwindled to just about no one. Just some gray-hairs who have lived here a long time, whose lives have bridged the unparalleled transition from then to now.

Ten years ago it seemed that half of Delaware County was for sale. This made it seem even lonelier then, as if you might easily find a hut and some work as a hoop shaver and be left in the silence you want. There were plenty of places to wander, and no one really minded. Now half of the county is owned by people who do not live there but instead come up for weekends from the city or New Jersey. (This sounds like an exaggeration but is not; tax maps show that more than half the houses in the county are owned by nonresidents.) It was all ripe for the plucking, we see now in hindsight blurred by a tear over its conversion from a place that we had discovered and was to remain ours, if only in our dreams. This forces everything else to change, because these are people not likely to be satisfied with the tired offerings of the Margaretville A&P or an early-bird dinner of spaghetti at the Inn Between. Not when the charms of the Catskills have been broadcast in the "Escapes" section of *The New York Times*, next to an equally admiring article on Aspen and across from a half-page ad for Land Rover. Now the distant fields and woodlots are dotted with smartly designed farmland interpretations of the International Style. The remaining villages are bustling again, with no place to park now, but these people do not know one another, do not depend on one another. They make nothing, farm nothing, produce nothing. They do not battle the weather; they leave. The insular walls have been breached, and history is leaking out from the gap, soaking into the ground.

Apparently, someone has ordained that the Catskills can no longer be themselves. They are going to wrestle them into submission, too. No longer a self-possessed place that decides for itself who can survive here, what animals will roam its mountains, it will be made comfortable for the comfortable. In the denatured Catskills of the future, an entire mountain will be shorn and regraded. The trucks will start arriving with deliveries of its new substance: whatever it is they use to make that fantastic green. When they wander out of their new condos and hotel rooms and get into their white electric carts to move as one with their small machines over the new golf courses that have been laid atop the mountain, the newcomers will not even know they are in the Catskills. And in a way, they won't be.

Wherever you go, it is coming to get you. (*You can't stop progress.*) For all of human history, it is joined to death as the only other thing that can never be avoided; taxes are more recent. Your job is to sit still and take it, and don't question where it comes from. It can take pretty much everything you really care about or that makes your life worth living, but don't complain or you will be a sniveler who doesn't understand the nature of things, the inevitability of the inevitable. Change is always called "progress" so you can't oppose it.

First is the land. Then the home on which it is placed. Both are situated on the continuum of loss. There is only either more or less, faster or slower, caused by individuals or caused by agglomerations of strangers equipped with laws. The desert view taken in 1872 by Timothy O'Sullivan and sold back east to astonished consumers of the sublime is rephotographed a hundred-some years on. Telephone wires and a ranch house fill the foreground. We don't care, so we don't stop it. We don't stop it, so we don't care.

John Keats, in 1956's *The Crack in the Picture Window* ("bitter, devastating"; "red-eyed with anger"; "a Highly Controversial Book"), called them "fresh-air slums." Then, they were new developments of rank upon rank of small houses for the working class, which wrecked forever the land upon which they were placed, and the lives of the people who were forced into debt to buy junk that enriched only the builders and sellers of it. Forty years later we have fresh-air slums consisting of huge consumerist nightmares for the well-to-do-without-taste-or-conscience. The lives of the people who buy them do not seem wrecked by them, but that is because they were prewrecked, or the wrecking consists of further numbing of the thoughtful mind by the sight of so many feet of granite kitchen counter. But these treeless streets also wreck the land and all that would otherwise live on it. And both were "vomited up" by developers, in Keats's felicitous turn of words.

How much more do we get, how much more do we have to take? Enough is not too much. Too much is when we're gone. There is not a power upon the earth that will stop progress. Except progress itself. When the air can't be breathed, when the psyche starts running amok from too many others crowding the elbow, when the spring comes four weeks too soon, when the floods come, when the trees wither, when the billion diverse creatures that weave together in ways we cannot comprehend to make the net that holds us up die, when selfishness calls the chickens home to roost, then it will stop. Too bad we won't be around to celebrate our triumph over ourselves at last.

THE LARGE AERATING fountain on the former site of Brown's Station has always been a favorite picnicking retreat for locals around the Ashokan Reservoir. The pine trees that were planted by the thousand on the land that was stripped have grown into a great dark canopy, and in the summer they offer marvelous shade intensified, when the breeze blows right, by a fine mist that comes off the plume of water shooting skyward. The fountain is no longer used to oxygenate the water for the purpose of improving taste and odor, but it would have been unseemly, another latter-day robbery, for the city to take it away from the people. So it has been retooled and left as the only place here that performs no other function than giving pleasure. In the recent absence of other safe places—no such thing as a little-traveled road anymore—small children first learn to ride their bicycles here. They may soon graduate to the paved walkway on top of the reservoir's dividing weir, but that will be all. Their parents can never let them actually *go* anywhere on their bikes, because it has become too dangerous. Since the past never reappears in the midst of the present, although we don't really know quite yet about the future, it does not look like the ever-hastening stream of cars will diminish. The population of Ulster County has been on the rise, sometimes steadily, sometimes spiking. The projection for the next twenty years is an increase of up to 20 percent. When such news appears in the papers, it has the effect of looking just like the items that surround it: the basketball team is going to the championships; the library is getting a much-needed makeover. But a chart showing that within county lines there are currently 5,702 new, proposed, or under-construction housing units—that these would incur approximately 39,914 additional daily car trips along local roads is an amateur planner's marginal notation inked later—does not really belong in a section called "Business Review & Forecast." It belongs in the part of the paper devoted to "What They Term 'Quality of Life' Is Pretty Much Everything—and Here Are the Plans to Make It Miserable."

After September 11, 2001, especially, real-estate offices anywhere within a three-hour drive of the city were flooded with New Yorkers hoping to become ex–New Yorkers, and since there were not enough houses for them in this relatively rural county, just about every road now rumbles with heavy equipment, and just about every town meeting is taken up with applications for subdivision.

Almost a century after the towns along the Esopus were taken, an informational kiosk was raised at the place they call the Panhandle, in the middle of a grassy circle under the wide sky that overspreads the Ashokan and the mountains that rise beyond it. A shingled roof protects the exhibits in which you read of the places that were lost, and of the great feats of engineering that brought clean water to the people who wanted it. The other reservoirs got their versions, too. A couple of years later they thought to place signs as near to all the twenty-six vanished communities as possible, so that you may be driving down the road and suddenly into view flashes a brown-and-yellow sign—*Former site of Arena*—and it seizes you strangely. *But there's nothing here!* and then it is gone again.

On a hillside that once was part of Learia Sprague's farm, where through the trees you can see a sparkle of liquid in the valley below, is a new Pepacton Cemetery, owned by New York City. Old stone walls disappear down the slope. The wind can get fierce up here, but when you are dead you are not too bothered by wind. In one quadrant are gathered the headstones and whatever else remained of ancestors of the East Branch so long forgotten there was no one to claim the money due on their reappearance to the surface. Their confreres from the West Branch are set down in another square. A whole day, or week or month, will go by. No one will visit them except a porcupine, bent on his own important business in the bushes.

A mile from the Ashokan I sit. Stone walls, too, climb partway up the steep hill across from me. As amazing as the fact that they were built at all is the one that some sort of animal used to be contained by them. I am as stupid about farming as most of us these days, but I would guess that only cows would view two feet of rock as a true impediment to freedom. And I am obviously ignorant of matters understood by developers, because I believed that the steepness of that rewooded incline would have prevented the placement of a new house there.

The sound of a bulldozer pressing into a living tree and pushing until it cracks is a particularly sickening one. Chainsaws going all day, punctuated by crashing, is not much more pleasant. A logging road will find new life as a driveway. Once upon a time only the king could place his fortifications on the highest ridge; now the king who owns an SUV can do the same. It seems to go against nature, but then so much does, lately. I don't think I will have the satisfaction of collaring one of the egos-on-a-stick who is planning to build his supersized mansion on the hill that was my solace, but if I did I would pummel him with a piece of Alan Devoe's 1937 *Phudd Hill*:

> They lie—these curved and molded masses of rugged earth—brooding in an ageless silence, baking their hummocked backs in the hot summer sun, shouldering the cold white weight of countless snows, existing immutable and eternal while the oaks and firs upon their slopes wither and die and are born again through the passage of myriad seasons. So green are these hills, and so round and so many, that they suggest the massive tumuli of some gigantic and immemorially ancient race of man. I have walked upon them and extracted from their timeless earthiness the profoundest peace which it is possible to know.

In fact I used to walk on them all the time, and tried again last night, as the darkness was settling in its ancient way on a hellishly cold winter evening. Up an old logging trail, no footprints on the snow but those belonging to rodents and the dog that's just ahead of me, but the sight of the ridge from which all trees have been ripped towered a little too insistently. I was looking at it but not really thinking about it—I was mainly trying not to slide on the ice all the way back down the hill on my ass and smash into a rock—and I had a flash of memory from two years before. I had managed to climb, in better weather, all the way to the top of the ridge opposite my house, where it was much steeper than here, and when I got there and immediately wondered how I was going to get down without breaking an ankle, I found a dog's collar. It was arresting evidence that another alien had breached this height, which seemed to belong solely to itself. Now, in what I had thought was the safe twilight of frigid January, a car drove through my sight line as I gazed up. This was in a different class than an old collar. It shook me all the way through. It was the watchman, inspecting—against what incursions I could not even guess—the "property," for that is what this majestically self-possessed place had become. There was nothing that needed protecting there yet, only scraped earth and boundary lines that had allowed successive buyers to flip forty-acre lots with views of two mountain ranges for increasingly outlandish amounts of money. As of last night, that's another place I can never go again. When they start building, the age-old dark of the hillside's night will be swept away in lights and noise and car exhaust. "Private property" trumps "the profoundest peace which it is possible to know."

I start my futile kicking, just for show. The town building inspector informs me that there are no regulations concerning building on a slope, no requirement to do environmental-impact statements for a single-family dwelling. I have no clever retorts, and the only thing that comes out of me, dumb though it is, is, "Well, that's America for you!" He is alarmed: "You wouldn't want anyone to tell you what you can do with your own land, would you?" I suspect he would not appreciate my belief that actually I would, since it has occurred to me that there is no such thing as "your own land," any more than there is one stitch in a sweater that can be removed without consequence. It is funny how the sound of the well digger foretells the final loss of a galaxy: we are some of the lucky ones, to still have our Milky Way when we step out on the back porch, but it is there only for a little while longer. Only a few more houses on our road, only a few more developments in New Paltz or Kingston, and it will be gone, after billions of years. You can practically count the days.

———

Yet I cannot but express my sorrow that the beauty of such landscapes are quickly passing away, the ravages of the axe are daily increasing, the most noble scenes are made desolate, and oftentimes scarcely credible in a civilized nation. The wayside is becoming shadeless, and another generation will behold spots, now called improvements, which as yet, generally destroy Nature's beauty without substituting that of art. This is regret rather than a complaint; such is the road society has to travel; it may lead to refinement in the end, but the traveler who sees the place of rest close at hand, dislikes the road that has so many necessary windings. Nature has spread for us a rich and delightful banquet. Shall we turn from it? We are still in Eden; the wall that shuts us out of the garden is our own ignorance and folly.

You can tell this was written a long time ago, in 1835 to be exact, because no one is this angrily eloquent anymore. Apparently no one even notices the absence, except for a couple of writers of unread environmental newsletters and the occasional crank who pens a letter to the editor. Few are really sure what they're upset about—is it the water? no, the birds?—and another writer in the next edition will soon call them "antidevelopment," which is about as bad as being called an atheist. We have facts and news items, but no Thomas Cole to be indignant about them, so they fall away to the recycling bin unfelt. His question is answered by our silence: yes, we shall turn from Nature's banquet, all right. If only we could dig up from the ground old Cole, the painter of the great river nearby and the Catskill Mountains beyond, to say himself to the builders on hillsides in today's Hudson River valley: "I despise the miserable creatures who destroy the beautiful works of nature wantonly and for a paltry gain."

Once the houses are there, everything that preceded them is gone. It does not come back, because progress does not have a reverse gear. Somewhere between 1835 and now, it happened, and we can no longer say we are in Eden. But it is not us who were expelled from it: we banished Eden ourselves.

(In the space of only thirty years, they built twenty-five thousand shopping malls in our fair land, which you must admit is quite the achievement. We managed to create an economy where goods are manufactured and put up for sale before anyone knows they are needed: if you build it, they will come. We have been perfecting this for a while now. What took a steel mill in 1850 an entire year to produce could be made in a day by 1900.)

> Now we have cause to love the reservoirs. Certainly, they have their own beauty: By moonlight the Ashokan Reservoir is a shimmering glory. The moon's soft mellowness gives to the ravines below and the peaks of surrounding mountains a tinge of loveliness that nothing else can approach. One exclaims with Maupassant: "Perhaps God has made such nights in order to throw a veil of idealism over the lives of men."

The view from Wittenberg Mountain that caused the author of *Our Catskill Mountains* to write swooning lines in 1931 is indeed splendid. In fact, it highlights the single thing that has preserved the view at all: the reservoir that took home from so many people has at last given back something.

The surrounding area still has more than a few farms, thanks mainly to the miracle of modern chemistry. Not for us, yet, the precedent of Vermont, which lost *90 percent* of its farms between 1950 and 1990. The hundreds of acres of cornfields that line the flats here along the Esopus are made profitable in part by the yellow crop duster that dives low on summer evenings to release a sudden fog, and give you a headache. The rich bottom-land has been a monoculture for so long it would not be possible to continue growing sweet corn summer after summer without either the relative inefficiencies of what used to be known as good stewardship of the soil or these economical chemical drenchings. Still, they are almost worth the preservation of the open space, and thus the residents' continuing ability to believe they live in a rural community. (Otherwise the sights would include ever more like what must be the last eight dairy cows in Ulster County, grazing under the shadow of six taupe McMansions hunkered on a slope of former meadow.) But it is the thousands of acres of uninhabited, forested land in the buffer zones of the New York City watershed that have preserved a wilderness in the midst of an inexorably creeping urbanization. You can literally watch it coming (hooray, satellite images!). It radiates out from the city, colored orange on the maps; Long Island has gone from green, in 1955, to all orange except at the very tip. It has moved outward to color much of Connecticut, New Jersey, the northern suburbs. It is moving up on an ancient target, the Highlands, or more precisely the Reading Prong, the northern reach of the Appalachian Mountains. This is predicted to reach "buildout" in another thirty years unless something can be done to protect it—unlikely, with the kind of development pressure placed against it, and the prices that keep rising and make it nearly impossible for conservation groups to buy large enough chunks to make a difference. And still, they are only chunks: when you break your favorite bowl, do you still have it if you keep the pieces?

KINGSTON IS AN amazement of a city. It is strung out like a necklace, three beads that used to be separate places. Uptown is a smaller Georgetown or Nantucket, with narrow streets curling around centuries-old houses that press up against one another. Some of the stone buildings, made by early Dutch settlers, predate 1700. Where Crown and John streets intersect, four eighteenth-century stone houses still stand on the corners, the only place in America where this is so. Uptown Kingston is like a museum that does not have many visitors, but people still live there, and you can walk down the streets and pretend you lived there a long time ago. There are more recent structures, too—representatives from every era when they took their architecture seriously, because it served a civic function and not just an expedient one—as well as the occasional old neon sign proclaiming the availability of Chop Suey within. This kind of continuity with another age makes one feel a deep contentment. Albany Avenue, which was once the address of choice for the Victorian gentleman who had made good—or very good indeed—has unfortunately been turned into a four-lane thoroughfare for getting from one business district to another. Nonetheless, the houses are well maintained, and occasionally vibrantly painted, in the multitudinous schemes apparently favored by designers of intricate woodwork. This is where you will find the funeral home, which is how you know you're among the finest houses a city has to offer. Behind a wall of evergreen bushes that does a good job of shielding it from the traffic is an older stone house—or mansion, if you will. I have long passed the age of party crashing, but I got a renewed opportunity last summer, and this is where I was led. Just off the avenue I had often sped down, behind the house in the middle of the city, spread a scene of such antique bucolic splendor I might have been standing in front of something at the Center for British Art instead. A long and narrow wooden staircase was necessary to descend a tangled hill of brush, and then I was on the greensward of a lord's country seat, an expanse of many acres of nothing but soft green lawn. A small lake was set like an opal in its midst, and a little island intruding into it housed the manor's sheep and goats. A fence forestalled their free range, which would have been a more authentic touch, but necessary after the sheep had been found one day some distance away on the grounds of the city museum called the Senate House (built in 1676 and one hundred years later the first meeting place of New York's state senate). I had read about the incident in the paper and wondered where in Kingston one might keep sheep; now I knew.

Downtown, along where the Rondout Creek meets the Hudson, is perhaps even more astonishing, with its nineteenth-century brick warehouses and large pieces of wilderness spilling down the steep embankments to be met by ragged remnants of human culture in the pre–Wal-Mart age. In other words, not much has changed here in a hundred years. Kingston Point Park had to be rescued from being reclaimed by the aforesaid wilderness—it had long before been the city's amusement park, with boating lagoons, a carousel, and the trolley line to bring crowds of pleasure seekers—but like much else in this part of town, it had fallen into the twilight of someone's dream. Forgotten for decades by everyone but the brambles, it was finally and partially rehabilitated by the Rotary Club in 1990. Now it is still largely forgotten, but it has gazebos on the heights of its rocky outcroppings, a delirious view of the Hudson, a bridge to walk across, benches to sit alone on and wonder, and a sense that this is a personal and very valuable gift. A few citizens who regularly bring their dogs here to play own it more than anyone, which is fine: they are often the only ones who stay, because the teenagers slouch down holding their radios, stand for a few minutes watching the huge weight of water moving itself and occasionally a barge or tanker inexorably downstream, then turn and depart. The dog people are on their own again.

Once upon a time there was a brickyard next to the park, just as once upon a time there were a lot of things going on on the riverfront. Now almost all, except for the junkyards, are gone. The shore of the river is littered with historic bits of brick. It is peaceful and lovely. Three hundred and sixty-three condos are being proposed for the brickyard. Another site just north of it has excited the attention of developers from Yonkers who think it should have some two thousand new units. The quiet park would be quiet no longer. It would not be possible to get close enough to it to visit. The dogs would have to have their fun at home. The old warehouses would become sports bars. Dunkin' Donuts would open a franchise, and three drugstores, representatives of the major chains, would open in contiguous spanking-new buildings, replacing a structure where boats were repaired, a ferry landing from back in the day, and the place where a popular broadsheet had been printed and history recorded. Good riddance. The street that quietly follows the contour of the creek and joins Kingston Point with its downtown kin, the business district that retains a whole block of Italianate facades with small stores, would be called upon to somehow support the insistent passage of thousands and thousands of cars. Since it could not do it without being destroyed, destroyed it will be. Kingston, along with its living remembrance of the age of chop suey, will be tossed into an unmarked grave.

THE MEMORY OF what happened to the old Ashokan places has not really died. It can be stirred back to full life pretty quickly. People were still watching on TV, for the first of their many, many times, the black smoke pouring from two great skyscrapers that yet stood in lower Manhattan when the three roadways across the reservoir were shut down by Department of Environmental Protection police. Two years later, one of them was still closed and would remain so, meaning that school buses and ambulances would have to take a longer and extremely curving route around the water. A demonstration was held in protest. Signs read FIRST DISPOSSESSED . . . NOW DISENFRANCHISED and OPEN THE DAM ROAD. A speaker told the small crowd, "About one hundred years ago, New York City and the town of Olive entered into a shotgun wedding. And the town of Olive has been the abused spouse ever since." Whenever the city buys additional property around its reservoirs— it is trying like anything to avoid having to build a filtration plant that will cost billions—the anger flares up anew. The city is in a strange position of telling people what they can and can't do with their land at the same time it is trying to make amends, and it has built a heck of a lot of new septic systems for homeowners in recent years. A DEP commissioner in the 1980s often visited the Catskill and Delaware watersheds to talk to residents, and said she found herself "fencing with ghosts."

With population surging, and more and more houses and offices, stores and hotels, churches and condos going up in every last lot in the countryside, the wooded acreage that filters water the natural way before it flows into the great cisterns is all that will be left uninhabited. Around the Croton System, in Westchester County much nearer the city, population grew 39 percent between 1970 and 1985, pretty much completing the job of full suburbanization. A letter writer to *The New York Times*'s Westchester section said that in the past few years he had seen "a significant deterioration in the quality of life: increased traffic, increased development, loss of open space," but he was glad for the reservoir system, "as an object of beauty and a brake on development, . . . a double blessing." Maybe not enough of one: more than three thousand acres (how many more could be left?) are currently slated for development. Westchester, in turn, is the canary in the mine for Ulster.

Can the museum be far behind? A design to commemorate the Catskill-Delaware watershed with permanent exhibits has been drawn. There would be a full-scale replica of the interior of the aqueduct, one hundred feet long. There would be "history walls," with artifacts and news clippings, and a "wall of appreciation" dedicated to those whose homes were taken. Of course, there would be a diorama, allowing big people to tower over the land made small. And the building's stone walls outside would "bleed water."

WE ADMIT TO BIAS, finally. For what we wish in intimate moments is for the world to shrink. It would have to unfurl the other way, backward in time, until so many people would return to nothingness, not a cruelty but rather the prevention of any possible occurrence of one. They would go back to when they were not even a hopeful sigh on a mother's lips. Then, so much might not be lost. We, in our terrible greed, could keep what had made us love it even without our meaning to: home as we know it.

Or another dream. During the change of countless seasons, the water spills down, and tiny grains are loosened. The drops seep in, then freeze. They thaw once more, and the cracks begin to show. Once they have managed to become small, they will become larger. They spread. Underneath was once earth, dirt that always carries seeds, though no one really sees how. As the green pushes upward, the weak bent on destroying the powerful, the cracks widen and proliferate. The oil stains become faint. Outside in the night, the wind gets under a piece of plastic. It has been mottled with dots of gray, filth or perhaps mold, something alive. It snaps and goes, flying into the yard where it will be covered by the dead leaves of the maple in another season or two. Rain will soften the soil and in a matter of time will submerge it. Although it had been made to never rot, never is not something the earth and its acids really understand. No one watches this process. The place has been abandoned. The maple sends its winged seeds floating through the air.

The patio is gone. The driveway can barely be seen. The cracks have veined the foundation, though not much stands on it anymore. There is no longer any inside and out, because the moon shines through where the roof used to be; it is now spread over several acres, blown away in individual tiles, where it has been more easily disguised by the brush. Even the acrylic carpet has started to sustain life. It is the promised land for colonies of vast competing insect interests.

The sun rises and sets, over and over. A picture now, if it could be taken, would show only strange colors in the ground and a few spots where things are reluctant to grow tall. But a lynx has lately been stepping quietly past the place where the hot tub used to be. And sometime soon a passerby will stop. The wind through the trees that always used to make him think of cars in the distance sounds now like a soothing song, the wind through the trees. He looks out at the pristine view: *Why, it is just as I remember.*

MAKING BOOK

THE LONELY CABIN IN THE DEEP WOODS DRAWS YOU TO IT

Back-to-the-soil literature was chanting its siren song long before Horace Greeley with a fine disregard of drought and flood, Indians, grasshoppers, and kindred annoyances, first urged youth to go West. Characters, costumes, and locality alter with the decades, but the theme is constant. The Dust Bowl is only the most spectacular disaster for which this brand of literature has been responsible.

—FREDERIC F. VAN DE WATER,
We're Still in the Country, 1938

IT SEEMS TO HAVE appeared in my closet one day. That's not how it was, of course, but I have no real memory from what secret dumping ground of family refuse I might have plucked my great treasure. It is an oil painting, unframed and with a ghostly false start on the back of the board, of a mill on a stream in a dark pine woods. A mountain rises behind it, doubling the frightful sense of deterrence Nature here declares. Don't ask me how I know, I just know, that no other habitation would show itself in the surrounds even if the edges of the picture were extended—forever—beyond their present eight by ten inches. There is no more evocative painting in the world; the loneliness sends a lovely shudder through you. In part that's due to the happy accident of time's acids, which have interacted with the oil colors to make them so dim that the mill seems to live in a perpetual coming of night.

And don't ask why no other cousin or sister seemed to care in the least that it was I who came into possession of such an alluring prize. I ought to be embarrassed to reveal that when I was younger I was convinced it was quite valuable and a museum curator would surely gasp and beg for it. I could gaze into it for years; I could insert myself into its imaginary space, and finally live where I have always wanted to live.

The Lonely Little Cabin/Mill/Farmstead in the Woods is a convention from way back; the little picture of it I have, probably painted by some great-great-great-aunt, is somewhere around ninety or a hundred years old. Even if our pioneer predecessors had not yet thought to hang a portrait of the idealized lonely cabin in their own actual lonely cabins, the next generation was quickly on the case. And so on down the years until every other Indiana ranch house sports a similar impossibly emotive painting over the sofa. For those with sufficient means, these are procured from a licensed Thomas Kinkade store (also lovely, dark and deep, paneled as they are with burnished if fake cherrywood and fitted out in forest green and brass lamps whose downglow conjures the welcoming mystery of an English manor, just steps from the hard glare of the mall corridor). Thomas Kinkade is the Painter of Light™, although these days he no longer has to paint the light himself. It is applied by trained specialists. They take the multitudinous "paintings" after they come off the production line and, according to some recipe known only to the anointed, dab actual yellow paint onto the windows and streetlamps of homey scenes that never existed except in mythic imaginings. These highlights send into some gathering gloom the message: in this house is warmth, cheer, the human antithesis of the inhuman loneliness without.

This particular person's cornering of the market of this particular artistic manifestation of our drive to feel okay in Creation, and the forbidding emotions that require the endeavor, is too easy a mark. Or at least he is if seen as the purveyor of cheap sentiment. But that light in the windows is very near a philosophical treatise. He is uncanny to codify it. The darkness makes necessary the light, and the light reiterates the dark. These are the two elements in which we live, or did, and they symbolize everything about us and the whole darn eternal struggle.[1]

The painter who sends a small glow into the dark from the bastion of human habitation has given emotional figuration to feelings that must have been a lot more common a while ago—*I wonder if we are winning this battle after all; it is breathlessly exquisite, this balance between night and day*—but that curiously persist though it is certain that the dark forces of nature have been vanquished once and for all. They must be persisting, or else a Thomas Kinkade franchise would not be worth what it is, and his lighthouses and commemorative plates and Christmas village scenes would not be advertised in millions of copies of *Ladies' Home Journal*. There is something tenaciously primitive about their appeal. It is raw and alarmingly simple, and it is what Thomas Hardy was getting at in his poem "The Fallow Deer at the Lonely House":

---

[1] "A hermit's hut. What a subject for an engraving!" So writes our old friend Gaston Bachelard; but he also warns the artist that the subject will "suffer from any exaggeration of picturesqueness." Take note, if you plan on attending the sale of "original Oil Paintings!" at the Hilton any time soon.

One without looks in tonight
Through the curtain chink
From the sheet of glistening white;
One without looks in tonight
As we sit and think
By the fender-brink.

We do not discern those eyes
Watching in the snow;
Lit by lamps of rosy dyes
We do not discern those eyes
Wondering, aglow,
Four-footed, tip-toe.

This is what we do, too, to these pictures: look in from outside, imagine the life of others, who are also us.

The analogous genre of books allows us finally indoors. The progenitor of this enduring line of lonely-cabin writings is, of course, *Walden*, which Henry David Thoreau began in 1846, detailing the building of a rustic hut by a pond and the year spent in it. That he even conceived of the project is testimony to the truism that you don't know what you've got till it's gone, or nearly so. When there is too much of it, the wilderness is the seat of chaotic evil (it's bad to "be-wilder"); but when it is threatened with ultimate extirpation, it becomes something to revere and preserve, an emblem of great goodness. The American conservation movement was just stirring to life in the mid-nineteenth century, after the artist George Catlin made the first plea for preservation in the form of a national park in 1832. The scent of impending eradication must have been in the air, for this was the same decade in which Alexis de Tocqueville surveyed the country and what it stood to lose: "It is the consciousness of destruction, of quick and inevitable change, that gives such a touching beauty to the solitudes of America. One sees them with a sort of melancholy pleasure; one is in some sort of hurry to admire them." This then is the

gesso on those paintings: the knowledge of certain loss. It under-
lies every picture of the solitary dwelling in the midst of terrible
beauty.

In 1893 the western frontier was called closed. There was
nowhere else to go but back, into the memory of prelapsarian life.
(Frederic Remington complained in 1900, "I shall never come to
the West again.—It is all brick buildings—derby hats and blue
overalls—it spoils my earlier illusions.") The first of these idylls
remains first in our hearts, because it was also no doubt first on
our reading lists: Laura Ingalls Wilder's *Little House in the Big
Woods*. Published in 1932, it was followed by eight other volumes
recounting the life of a pioneer girl in the barely tamed America
of the last three decades of the nineteenth century. Read it again
after forty years, and the words leap up with eidetic strength:
ohmigosh, I remember that! And you realize you have been carrying with you all this time just under your consciousness the picture of the attic filled with pumpkins and put-away food, dried
and salted. ("Often the wind howled outside with a cold and lonesome sound.") The book is both as specific as iron nails and as
universal as poetry; it is written with a lovely economy that is
wholly appropriate to its subject, which is life that is stripped
down but suggestively rich: "All the cousins were told to kiss Mary
and Laura, so they did." A sentence like that contains a whole
paragraph's worth of explanation of era-specific social behavior,
but the book has no use for prolixity. It is a child's vivid recollection
of the things that made an impact on a child's sight, and so they did
on ours, aided by Garth Williams's pencil drawings. Not that
without a picture you couldn't have just as precisely pictured the
hollow tree trunk used for a smokehouse, with its little roof above
and door below—for some reason you never forget that it had
leather hinges. Maybe because everything is an amazement; everything makes you cognizant of the pure ingenuity of human beings
who had to make a living for themselves (who *could* make a living
for themselves) alone in the middle of the woods, miles from
anyone. Laura is already a little girl before she ever sees a town, a

tiny one at that. But by page six she is teaching you how to put away venison for the winter, and later how to make lead bullets. There was a use for everything, including what was left over after another use: the oat straw is woven into hats, and the bladder of a slaughtered pig becomes a balloon for the children. It should make anyone who frequents Toys "R" Us positively blanch.

Only upon rereading the book as an adult are you conscious enough to realize that in this one volume is a universe of knowledge, and this knowledge has now been lost.[2] It is enough to set you weeping, or out into the woods for yourself. Indeed, this kind of motivator is what the genre was shortly to become.

This "to-the-land" book appeared at a time when "back-to-the-land" was an idea ready to be born. In fact, it was the year *Little House* was published that Helen and Scott Nearing moved to rural Vermont from the city in order to put into practice the theories of life as it should be lived, which they felt were being opposed by "a social order activated by greed and functioning through exploitation, acquisition and accumulation." In other words, Helen Nearing's *Living the Good Life* is not a humorous look at homesteading. That belongs to the other vein in this literary class. But it did have a profound impact on future generations.

At times it can be hard to see why. They never cheated on their beliefs, and their beliefs were strict. They gave away any surplus to friends and strangers, even thrusting produce at people on the streets of New York City. They believed building wooden houses in a land of plentiful stone was an example of American laziness, and never left home without bringing back a rock. When they sold a log cabin they had built by hand in order to learn how to do it, they priced it at materials and labor alone, for

---

[2] To save this ancient information was the impetus behind the *Foxfire* books, which began in 1966 as a high-school English class project in the Georgia Appalachians. Thus if necessary we may find out how to make white oak splits, soap, chairs, straw mattresses, butter, log cabins, wagons, moonshine. Or we may just marvel that somewhere, somehow, long, long ago people figured out how to do these things, and passed the knowledge on. Until it stopped dead, in our lifetime.

profit was anathema to them. They have no funny stories about wayward farm animals, because they refused to exploit them, too. Unlike others' books, theirs contains no down-home recipes; she offers food to her guests along the lines of "raw cauliflower and boiled wheat." It is left to the reader to decide whether the resulting good health that led them to enjoy two decades without ever having to see a doctor is worth the menu. But guests came, and guests stayed, at the home of the pied pipers of what would become a short-lived burst of commune building.

Later books would carry some of the manifesto tone, if not the sharp determinedness, of the Nearings' short temper with American attitudes. Helen Hoover and her husband moved to the far northern woods of Minnesota in 1954. Would that they had taken *Little House in the Big Woods* with them. Then they might have done as every self-respecting pioneer did: start a vegetable garden first thing. And so they wouldn't have come down with scurvy, or lain in bed for a week with a deadly infection, or become so fatigued with malnutrition it was hard to work. For all her belief that they were coming to live in harmony with the natural world, they are rather more like nosy interlopers, relying on mail-ordered food and others to deliver it, no one to steal it, and the weather to cooperate in allowing it through, none of which can be relied on.[3] Perhaps only someone who does not in fact "live"

---

[3] Another book that would have benefited them, had it been written yet, is *Wilderness Wife*, 1976, by Bradford and Vena Angier, or any number of the prolific Bradford's earlier outdoor manuals: *Field Guide to Edible Wild Plants, Survival with Style, Feasting Free on Wild Edibles, How to Live in the Woods on Pennies a Day.* No vitamin deficiencies when you know where grow the fiddleheads, dandelions, and nettles. ("'Ummm,' I enthused, knowing that protein-rich nettles are among the most versatile and potentially valuable of all plants.") This memoir is almost as annoying as Hoover's, but for the opposite reason—these folks are altogether *too* capable. They go out and shoot a bull moose for dinner, then decide on the spur of the moment to spend the night out in the British Columbia woods, no matter that it is snowing. Or that they have no shelter. In a half hour, he's built one for them out of a poplar sapling and spruce boughs. They settle down to moose kabobs that include small wild onions "from a patch Brad had found deep in the windswept sand on the shore" and then pass a night that she declares "one of the snuggest I have ever spent, although we learned later . . . that the temperature had plummeted far below zero."

from the land—instead, they are writer (she the author of 1966's widely read *The Gift of the Deer*) and illustrator—can be so sanctimonious about "protecting" it. So they name and feed visiting lynx, squirrels, and groundhogs and allow the wildlife to feast in their garden once they do attempt one. Often they disdain the proper tools, and so waste their energy; they lack the money for decent heat, even though they are in the midst of a forest that could provide ample fuel.

In *The Years of the Forest*, Hoover's 1973 account of the years 1956 to 1967, she writes of her affront that they are shunned as kooks by some of the locals. But there is no getting around it. They *are* kooks. Helen Hoover judges nearly everyone; surely she can stand a little judging in return. Nonetheless she is bent on educating her reader to the things that matter: she stands behind a lectern to deliver papers on "timeless things—life, death, eternity, and time itself," in which she boldly calls them the items "we so often forget when we lose sight of our place in the scheme of nature." But one has to wonder if our place is in fact providing graham crackers for the local rodents. Beyond these philosophical quibbles, pedantry simply makes for less interesting reading than depictions of the often extraordinary travails of living, as we say now, off the grid. Early in the book we are made expectant by the gripping story of one of the first tasks the Hoovers undertook in their new house: the filling of knotholes in the floorboards. It is actually awe-inspiring to read how they figured out that a previous denizen's tin patches for the holes were gathering the cold, which turned to frost during winter nights, then held melted moisture when warmed in the day against the boards and led to dry rot. (This is the kind of complex system that often hides behind the simplest aspect of wilderness life, as we see to our pleasure over and over again.) Turns out the floorboards had been laid wrong side up, so that the natural taper of a knothole, which would otherwise hold in a plug, caused it to fall to the basement instead. The fix for this little problem is about as convoluted as the explanation.

It is unfortunate that this story provides the exception in the book. For incredible hardships told with an ear to what readers most want in a homesteading memoir, you need to read *We Took to the Woods*. Louise Dickinson Rich's 1942 tale of life with her husband (and later the baby she delivered by herself) in the northwesternmost bit of Maine is clearly the model for many later books, even to the casual theft of her title—though without its lovely pun—for use in numberless chapter titles, flap copy, blurbs. What cannot be stolen is the writer's voice, which is as engaging as any you'd care to hear. She understands a basic truth: nothing interests humans more than reading about how humans really live—how they stay warm, what they eat, and, of course, where they go to the bathroom.

Here we might note that the majority of back-to-the-land memoirs during this period are written by women. And why should this be? The bald fact is that often the male half was back in the city, working as doctor or ad man to get the money to pay for the rundown farm and outfit it with the appropriate livestock. Or if it was he who spearheaded the move to the frontier, he was too busy justifying it by chopping firewood and fixing engines. Certainly, some of these literary products were another output, like jam or knitted socks, that enabled the family to stay solvent in the backwoods.

Rich makes it easy to appraise her situation as heaven, since there is no road (though they possess five cars) to their house. Instead, they have a river. But how many would continue thinking in that line if it were they, and not Louise, who gave birth in a bed in the unheated summer house on December 18 when it was ten below zero outside? There is a charming genuineness in that and all her descriptions. In one she tells of felling a tree in the snowy woods with a two-man saw, "with the lavender shadows of the bare trees lying like lace on the snow," and you're grateful for the transporting nature of purely episodic prose working on essential matter.

Indeed, what they go to the woods to experience—the self

"in nature"—is not a choice, it is a need. It is a need we have for some reason pretended we did not need, and that is the imperative of these stories. The reason we have sought to pretend is also foregrounded in them: the terrible adversity nature presents to all who dwell in it fills us with the wish, or delusion, to believe we actually have some say in our relationship with it.

Now we talk of making a "return." To what, then? It is clear these missives from the back of beyond are reporting on the Quest That Will Make Us Whole—away from where we are, back to what we were. It is a universal impulse to long for childhood once it is irrevocably lost, and the wilderness offers a way to retrieve the childhood of man: The illuminating Yi-Fu Tuan says in *Topophilia*, "The sylvan environment was . . . the warm nurturing womb out of which the hominids were to emerge. Today the cabin in the forest clearing remains a powerful lure to the modern man who dreams of withdrawal." This particular dream consists of a longing to live in the moment, as the practitioners of American cut-rate Buddhism would have it, a longing to provide for oneself. The result will restore us to our elemental selves, as animals. The relief this offers to those who attempt it is that the difficulties, thank god, are all external.

And sometimes difficult in the extreme. There are the bears, and there is the weather. It is no surprise to find a preoccupation with thermometer readings in almost all of these books— ten, twenty, even sixty below zero reported, and still the water must be brought in from outside. The woodstove becomes a main character in the drama. Indeed, in the most humorous of all these tales ("A Riot of Laughs" opined the *Washington Star*), Betty Mac- Donald's *The Egg and I*, "Stove" is a major presence with as much personality as the neighbors, the Kettles and the Hicks. A best- seller from its publication in 1945, the book tells of a young wife's sojourn on a previously abandoned farm in the Pacific Northwest. The whole ordeal is played for laughs. Of going into chicken farming, she asks plaintively, "Why has it become the common man's Holy Grail?" The answer, obviously, is that they were in such a hurry to get to the poultry chapter of *Five Acres and Independence* (twenty-three printings in the decade after publication in 1935) that they missed the part in "Tried and True Ways to Fail" on "chicken fever": "the one greatest trap for the unwary." The USDA agriculturist and author M. G. Kains wrote in his own plaintive way, "Just why so many inexperienced people think there is an easy and profitable business in poultry keeping is a minor phenomenon."

No matter. It gives Mr. MacDonald something to do, and gives Betty a classic Education of a Farm Wife: "I learned the inadequacy of 'Oh, dear!' and 'My goodness!' and the full self-satisfying savor of sonofabitch and bastard rolled around on the tongue."

The chapters relate all the standard themes: bizarre neighbors, difficulties of sustaining a water supply, heat that's never hot enough, the inscrutable domesticated animal, and Canning: Why It Is Universally Loathed and Feared. Her pressure cooker bursts, at no small danger to her, but still "I was lyrical with joy. . . . After supper I went humming about the house picking pieces of chicken off the picture frames and from the mirror in the bedroom." Whereupon her husband decides to get her a bigger, better pressure cooker.

Although the whole sunny affair (which you know was less than charming before her pen got to it) gets a swift kick in the gut by her portrayal of the native people as "shifty-eyed" and ignorant, dirty and ignominious, it remains armchair traveling at its finest. You visit your own country made strange. And since all struggles are resolved in high good spirits, you may maintain illusions that someday, when you get the chance, you're going to buy a derelict farm, too.

If one exists. *The Egg and I* is an exception among its group in neither witnessing nor lamenting the encroachment of "civilization," in the form of roads, houses, tourists, logging operations, and every other form of fragmentation. Even the Ingalls family experiences it. The motivation behind the move to the midwestern prairie that is detailed in the third book of the series, *Little House on the Prairie*, is that "Pa said there were too many people in the Big Woods now." This might serve as a letdown to those of us entirely susceptible to the back-to-land genre's main talking point, that at some finite time the world became overpopulated and caused that inborn need for lonely space to kick in. But it is finally a reminder, once again, that everything is relative: population rises on a curve, and always has. How many people is too many? Pa felt it was too crowded in 1882, so there.

Nonetheless it is often heartbreaking to spend two hundred pages in solitude only to wake the next to the sound of chainsaws and shouts. The work of staying alive in the wilderness frequently is met by the work of staying in the wilderness. The Hoovers contended with this loss, as did the Angiers, and one writer—Anne LaBastille, author of *Woodswoman*, 1976, a strident and clichéd account of hand-building a cabin in the Adirondacks—spends an entire book fending off humans who disturb her solitude.

But in 1951, it was still possible to be as lonely, if not altogether alone, as one wished—even in Dutchess County, a mere seventy miles from Manhattan. Helen Train Hilles's *Farm Wanted* reads like a template for a certain subset of I-learned-the-hard-way comic memoirs. It is never mentioned, but it is certain the author attended Wellesley/Smith/Vassar; she attends to the foibles of her overambitious citified husband; she is not above revealing an embarrassing personal anecdote to further the *Green Acres* story line; and she is unable to stanch the flow of recipes. Indeed, what does a farm wife do but cook—make do and cook? Thus Train Hilles offers "whole onion soup," in which the garden's oversupply of Spanish onions can be taken care of. (Best served with homemade croutons, thus doing in the stale bread, too.) You might think there would be little room for any storytelling besides these recipes in paragraph form, but she manages to pack any number into her narrative and never overwhelm the reader: *Zakuski*, a Russian cucumber appetizer good for removing surplus cucumbers; "white wine cup" (ditto); Pennsylvania Dutch relish; zucchini with Parmesan; red pepper puree; the ideal pig swill (for the pigs); and a whole menu starring homemade cottage cheese as the centerpiece. You quickly learn not to take her recommendations lightly: I'd look for Golden Bantam corn, if I were you. And still she manages to make reference to Lilly Daché hats, confirm the old wives' tale that says raw milk will go sour in a thunderstorm, relate the disturbing outcome of her sow's autopsy (blackberry taking root in the stomach), and detail what can be accomplished with white and black paint in fixing up decrepit chicken coops and steel drums meant for grain bins.

You know it is another era entirely when you read that the two-child Hilles family ventured into cow keeping in order to reduce their monthly milk bill. They move on to chickens. They learn, first and foremost, what will grow in their garden, and then how to grow what they will want to eat. (A successful kitchen garden is actually a type of miracle.) They learn all *sorts* of things, and this reiterates the fundamental interest of these books to the rest of us who lean longingly against the fence separating us from our own heritage—they are catalogs of what is learned, almost always the hard way. Would you know, anymore, how to locate the elderberry bush on your new old place, where to find watercress on the hoof? Whether or not it is overtly mentioned, this mode of living and learning is a way of disconnecting—using a kind of situational screwdriver—from the compulsions of capitalism. Look, you got a stream, you got mint; bunches of it placed among the winter blankets discourage the mice, and it's out there for the taking, no need for a trip to the store to purchase mothballs that poison you, for a price.

Notwithstanding the political theory, the expression of a particularly sardonic humor comes naturally with this territory. The author of *Farm Wanted* offers that "there seems to be more literature on the growing of horse-radish than the subject warrants." The chapter on canning is, of course, titled "Put Up or Shut Up."

Train Hilles's sister-in-arms is Marguerite Hurrey Wolf, who trades life as a doctor's wife in New York—"We lived in an apartment in mid-Manhattan where the car appeared automatically when summoned on the house phone, and the elevator operators considered dogs to be more chic than children"—for a summer farm in Vermont. She writes in *I'll Take the Back Road,* her 1965 collection of essays, "We came to Vermont because of a yearning to balance our dependent and mechanized winter life with the more self-reliant and simpler pattern of country ways." (Though "simpler" is rarely evidenced in these tales, since getting your living from the land has more steps than any uptown charity ball.) This reiteration of Thoreau's "We need the tonic of wildness" rationale for moving is pretty much her last straightforward statement. Then she, too, goes into the dry-humor mode favored by these well-educated and -tempered ladies of the farm: buying a seventeen-acre homestead "provided the children with cheap vacations and an enviable source of 'experience-sharing' discussions at school. It gave their parents aching backs, calloused hands, and a string of funny anecdotes with which to bore their friends all winter." But we are not bored. We press our noses against the glass and wish ourselves inside the cabin's warm embrace, even as we know that there is no real going back. The loss of how we used to be—made from the materials of how we used to live—must simply be borne. We are too far gone.

Yet it is only the most melancholy among us who can read books like these and find the humor and excitement of the narrative sliding right off the surface of the experience. It doesn't stick for us because we are all too aware that the passage of thirty, forty, fifty years cannot have been kind to the landscapes so lovingly described. The land is, in all cases, an even greater presence than Stove. I wonder if most of those who covet a Thomas Kinkade for the living room think much about the fact that the base on which his spun-sugar confections rise is all but gone. Perhaps we stand so distant from the possibility of living in true solitude in the midst of what we call "nature" but once was the world that it no longer seems even noteworthy that the symbols are all we have left. These books cannot be written anymore. (There is an end to that, too.) Like the unpeopled spaces they were born in, an entire genre of literature has been crowded out of existence. Not only because there are few "wildernesses" left to escape to—the South Pole, it turns out, now has a gift shop, and the Americans are planning to build a nine-hundred-mile road to connect it vehicularly to the nearest town, leaving a British explorer to muse that outer space is the only thing left to explore. No one can write a typical account of life in the lonely cabin now because to even think to write one is to believe that there is a future to the project. But that future, like solitude on a planet that is soon expected to somehow absorb nearly five billion more humans, is definitively gone. It turns out there *was* a finite time when the seesaw tipped forever to one end: since 1950, there has been more population growth than during the previous four million years. From now on we can be treated to no more fundamentally optimistic diaries of living alone in the woods. Instead, we see printed what must be the most dumbfounding example of how things have changed: an ad for Toyota's largest SUV, set against a background of a roadless topographical map. A faux wayside marker directs the driver, "Take so many people to the middle of nowhere that it becomes somewhere." The little cabin is no longer lonely, and it is no longer in the woods.

So DREAMS TURN INWARD. In a car driving through nighttime Pennsylvania, we are always coming into a succession of small towns with one traffic signal. The railroad tracks bump under the tires. The houses get closer together. We pass the strip. The grocery is still open. The diner is closed. There's the Pep Boys, a donut shop that is not a Dunkin' Donuts, a bar, a collision repair, a wedding-dress shop, another bar, a movie theater that is a movie theater. We seem to have come to the frontier. By the time we have reached mainly houses again, you are feeling nostalgia and the first tinglings of the tearing sensation that accompanies leaving home. The lights in the windows behind polyester lace curtains begin trying to slow the car. From outside, yellow light spilling into dark yards, it seems certain life inside these homes is gentle and explicable and happily self-contained, and this you want for yourself. There are no people in these pictures, ever, only four enclosing walls and the glow from the windows that is so sweetly sad it could break the heart of mankind. Each is a lonely little cabin, fundamentally unknowable. In the darkness outside, we pass by unseen, having imagined the lives of others, who are also us. And then drive out of town.

A COMMONPLACE BOOK OF HOME

Winston Churchill put it in a nutshell when he said, "We shape our dwellings, and afterwards our dwellings shape us."

———

"All thoughtful persons worry about the future of the children who will have to spend their lives under the absurd social and environmental conditions we are thoughtlessly creating; even more disturbing is the fact that the physical and mental characteristics of mankind are being shaped now by dirty skies and cluttered streets, anonymous high rises and amorphous urban sprawl, social attitudes which are more concerned with things than with men."

—RENÉ DUBOS, *So Human an Animal*, 1968

"Place absorbs our earliest notice and attention, it bestows on us our original awareness; and our critical powers spring up from the study of it and the growth of experience inside it. . . . One place comprehended can make us understand other places better."

—EUDORA WELTY, "Place in Fiction," 1956

———

"Every human advance is accompanied by a rent increase."

—GEORGES DARIEN, ca. 1910

———

"When one breaks camp in the morning, he turns back again and again to see what he has left. Surely he feels he has forgotten something; what is it? But it is only his sad thoughts and musings he has left, the fragment of his life he has lived there. Where he hung his coat on the tree, where he slept on the boughs, where he made his coffee or broiled his trout over the coals, where he drank again and again at the little brown pool in the spring run, where he looked long and long up into the whispering branches overhead, he has left what he cannot bring with him,—the flame and the ashes of himself."

—JOHN BURROUGHS, "Pepacton: A Summer Voyage," 1881

———

"A striking landscape is the skeleton upon which many primitive races erect their socially important myths. Common memories of the 'home town' were often the first and easiest point of contact between lonely soldiers during the war.

"A good environmental image gives its possessor an important sense of emotional security. He can establish an harmonious relationship between himself and the outside world. This is the obverse of the fear that comes with disorientation; it means that the sweet sense of home is strongest when home is not only familiar but distinctive as well."

—KEVIN LYNCH, *The Image of the City*, 1960

———

"This is the true nature of home. It is the place of Peace; the shelter, not only from all injury, but from all terror, doubt, and division."

—JOHN RUSKIN, 1856

———

"There are to be found in different parts of the country many families who have been settled for several generations on the same spot, and their old, simple wooden homesteads, mended and patched every few years, hold their own with commendable pertinacity. They have no idea of falling to pieces, and are altogether too substantial to be pulled down. Now this quality of durability is, of course, in the abstract, an excellent virtue for a house to possess; but it must be confessed that, in such very awkward and ungainly structures as often fall to the lot of these well-settled families, its presence could be cheerfully dispensed with, were it not for the many interesting associations and family reminiscences that linger round the old house, which has been, perhaps, the home of the father's and grandfather's childhood. These associations are so valuable, and so little fostered by the ordinary course of events in American families, that they deserve to be cherished in every possible way."

—CALVERT VAUX, *Villas and Cottages*, 1857

———

"It is well-nigh criminal to destroy or to undo great works of art and architecture which embody the product of the labor and the genius of so many men of so many ages. It is like nullifying the lives of so many generations of men—like obliterating them from the scroll of time—so far as their productive labors are concerned. It is like setting back the calendar of years to the time before those works were made, and creating a condition the same as if the works had never been performed. It is depriving the world of what makes for civilization and of what civilization is entitled to have, namely, the accumulation of the best products of human genius of all preceding generations."

—*Nineteenth Annual Report of the American Scenic and Historic Preservation Society*, 1914 (in *The American Environment: Readings in the History of Conservation*, ed. Roderick Nash)

———

"I wonder, too, if all the houses [my son] ever reads about in books will be this house, just as all the houses I read about are in the end the house in which I grew up. It was a low, white, old-fashioned house, and some of the houses in books are huge mansions. But no matter how carefully the author explains the arrangement of the rooms, no matter if he goes to the trouble of drawing a floor plan, when his characters go from the drawing-room down long corridors into the dining hall, in my mind's eye they pass from our little living room through a door to the left directly into the low square room where we ate."

—LOUISE DICKINSON RICH, *We Took to the Woods*, 1942

———

"The deeper the map [the "cognitive map" laid down in the brain the first time one sees a place] is engraved in our memory, the better it will resist the deterioration. . . . My oldest cognitive map, that of the village of my childhood encoded over sixty years ago, is still more vivid and more detailed in my mind than my maps of places where I lived only twenty years ago. If you look back at your life, you will probably find that your own childhood cognitive maps have the same astonishing clarity, even after many years."

—ERIK JONSSON, *Inner Navigation*, 2002

{February 26, 2004}

From the first time I heard the old sea chanty "Shenandoah" I thought it was about longing to go back to a place, then I found out that's not true. Then again, maybe it is. We are all forced to leave home, even if we never do, and

> Oh Shenandoah, I'm bound to leave you,
>
> Away, you rolling river.
>
> Oh Shenandoah, I'll not deceive you
>
> Away, I'm bound to go,
>
> Cross the wide Missouri.

The music swells and moves like a river. Is there anyone who hearing it does not cry?

> Carry me back to old Virginny,
>
> There's where the cotton and the corn and taters grow;
>
> There's where the birds warble sweet in the springtime,
>
> There's where this old darky's heart am long'd to go,
>
> There's where I labor'd all day in the cotton,
>
> There's where I worked in the fields of yellow corn,
>
> No place on earth do I love more sincerely,
>
> Than old Virginny, the state where I was born.

That was written by James Bland in 1880. Then in the twenties the Carter Family sang, "Carry me back to old Virginny, back to my Clinch Mountain home," because it's all really part of the same song, one big old-time blues ballad/spiritual/love song about longing for a place that feels like it's part of you and you're part of it.

"There is a reason that human beings long for a sense of permanence. This longing is not limited to children, for it touches the profoundest aspects of our existence: that life is short, fraught with uncertainty, and sometimes tragic. We know not where we come from, still less where we are going, and to keep from going crazy while we are here, we want to feel that we truly belong to a specific part of the world."

—JAMES HOWARD KUNSTLER,
The Geography of Nowhere, 1993

———

"All of our worlds die with us. This is either the eternal human tragedy or, because of its very inevitability, nothing worth fretting over."

—review of Patrick J. Buchanan's *The Death of the West: How Dying Populations and Immigrant Invasions Imperil Our Country and Civilization [!]* by BRIAN DOHERTY, *The Guardian Weekly*, February 6, 2002

———

"More roads were made, and the countryside was divided into lots. More houses and bigger houses . . . apartment houses and tenement houses . . . schools . . . stores . . . and garages spread over the land and crowded around the Little House. No one wanted to live in her and take care of her any more. She couldn't be sold for gold or silver, so she just stayed there and watched."

—VIRGINIA LEE BURTON, *The Little House:
Her-Story*, 1942

———

"If I had chosen to be born, I probably should not have selected Kinsman, Ohio, for that honor. . . . And yet my mind continuously returns to the old place, although not more than five or six that were once my schoolmates are still outside the churchyard gate. My mind goes back to Kinsman because I lived there in childhood, and to me it was once centre of the world, and however far I have roamed since then it has never fully lost that place in the storehouse of miscellaneous memories gathered along the path of life."

—CLARENCE DARROW, *The Story of My Life*, 1932

{January 28, 2002}

Is it related to how stuck we are to home, that particular thrill of hitting the road? It's almost illicit. I had a frisson of it here, in the diner attached to the Kingston Kmart, through the bizarre agency of a glass of grapefruit juice. I raised it to my mouth, and it touched and flowed, bringing with it the taste of the tin can in which it was lately housed. That one sensation instantly conjured a million mornings in cheap hotel dining rooms: Outside was the car or better yet the bike, and a road that went on to someplace so amazing it had to keep its identity hidden forever.

"I want to go to OUR house," wails Raphael at age two.

"But genius is only *childhood recaptured* at will, a childhood now equipped, in order to express itself, with virile organs and an analytical capacity that permits it to order all the matter it has involuntarily amassed."

—BAUDELAIRE, "The Painter of Modern Life," 1859

{undated}

Recall how, when you fell in what you believed was love with one of those ridiculous and now faceless crushes in that former life of yours, the first thing you wanted to do was take him home with you. You wanted to introduce the two, and hoped they would like each other. It would form some sort of test: would he feel the terrace under the maple in summer at cocktail hour was the most sublime place he had yet been?

———

My childhood's home I see again,
        And sadden with the view;
And still, as memory crowds my brain,
        There's pleasure in it too.

O Memory! Thou midway world
        'Twixt earth and paradise
Where things decayed and loved ones lost
        In dreamy shadows rise

And, freed from all that's earthly vile,
        Seem hallowed, pure and bright,
Like scenes in some enchanted isle
        All bathed in liquid light.

—ABRAHAM LINCOLN,
"The Return," 1846

———

How dear to this heart are the scenes of my childhood,
When fond recollection presents them to view.

—SAMUEL WOODWORTH,
"The Old Oaken Bucket," 1818

———

Where Thou art—that—is Home.

—EMILY DICKINSON, 1863

———

It doesn't matter at all if my home's big or small,
If it's brown or yellow or white;

It doesn't matter at all if it's narrow or tall,
Or if it's pretty or bright.

It doesn't matter at all if my home's on a hill,
Or down by the deep blue sea

—RENEE BARTKOWSKI,
My Home ("A Little Golden Book"), 1971

———

But now, alas, those scenes exist no more;
The pride of life with thee, like mine, is o'er,
Thy pleasing spots to which fond memory clings,
Sweet cooling shades and soft refreshing springs.
And though fate's pleased to lay their beauties by
In a dark corner of obscurity,
As fair and sweet they bloomed thy plaines among,
As bloom those Edens by the poets sung,
Now all's laid waste by desolation's hand,
Whose cursed weapons level half the land.
Oh who could see my dear green willows fall,
What feeling heart but dropped a tear for all?
Accursed wealth, o'erbounding human laws,
Of every evil thou remainst the cause.

—JOHN CLARE, "Helpstone," 1820

———

We shall not cease from exploration
And the end of all our exploring
Will be to arrive where we started
And know the place for the first time.

—T. S. ELIOT, "Little Gidding," 1943

―――――

"At night, when the streets of your cities and villages are silent and you think them deserted, they will throng with the returning hosts that once filled them and still love this beautiful land. The White Man will never be alone."

—CHIEF SEATTLE, 1854

―――――

"RANYEVSKAYA. . . . I love this house. Without the cherry orchard I can't make sense of my life, and if it really has to be sold, then sell me along with it."

—ANTON CHEKHOV, *The Cherry Orchard*, 1903

―――――

"EMILY (*softly, more in wonder than in grief*). I can't bear it. They're so young and beautiful. Why did they ever have to get old? Mama, I'm here. I'm grown up. I love you all, everything.—I can't look at everything hard enough. There's the butternut tree. (*She wanders up Main Street*) There's Mr. Morgan's drugstore. And there's the High School, forever and ever, and ever. And there's the Congregational Church where I got married. Oh, dear. Oh, dear. Oh, dear!"

—THORNTON WILDER, *Our Town*, 1938

―――――

"It was as old-fashioned as it was small, and it rested in the lap of an undulating upland adjoining the North Wessex downs. Old as it was, however, the well-shaft was probably the only relic of the local history that remained absolutely unchanged. Many of the thatched and dormered dwelling-houses had been pulled down of late years, and many trees felled on the green. Above all, the original church, hump-backed, wood-turreted, and quaintly hipped, had been taken down, and either cracked up into heaps of road-metal in the lane, or utilized as pig-sty walls, garden seats, guard-stones to fences, and rockeries in the flower-beds of the neighbourhood. In place of it a tall new building of modern Gothic design, unfamiliar to English eyes, had been erected on a new piece of ground by a certain obliterator of historic records who had run down from London and back in a day. The site whereon so long had stood the ancient temple to the Christian divinities was not even recorded on the green and level grass-plot that had immemorially been the churchyard, the obliterated graves being commemorated by eighteen-penny cast-iron crosses warranted to last five years."

—THOMAS HARDY, *Jude the Obscure*, 1895

---

atopos (Gr.), "no place": strange, bizarre
Unheimlichkeit (Ger.): feeling anxiously not-at-home
homesickness: [loaded, that one]
separation anxiety: for dogs, an intense hysteria when left alone by the mobile "home," i.e., you; for people, a panic that starts in the gut and may lead to faintness or nausea upon recognizing we are not at home, in whatever sense

---

Home is a map to life, quite literally for the Dogon of Mali. The house is laid out humanly: north-facing entrance vestibule is the male, with the door his sexual organ; female genitals are the door between the entrance and the center room, in which the woman does her spinning and weaving work. The couple sleeps here, and thus procreates here too. She also does her birth laboring here, facing away from the entrance. In *The Houses of Mankind*, Colin Duly explains, "Thus the child collects its life spirit, *nyama*, in the place where it was conceived."

"This is the most beautiful place on earth.

"There are many such places. Every man, every woman, carries in heart and mind the image of the ideal place, the right place, the one true home, known or unknown, actual or visionary. A houseboat in Kashmir, a view down Atlantic Avenue in Brooklyn, a gray gothic farmhouse two stories high at the end of a red dog road in the Allegheny Mountains, a cabin on the shore of a blue lake in spruce and fir country, a greasy alley near the Hoboken waterfront, or even, possibly, for those of a less demanding sensibility, the world to be seen from a comfortable apartment high in the tender, velvety smog of Manhattan, Chicago, Paris, Tokyo, Rio or Rome—there's no limit to the human capacity for the homing sentiment. Theologians, sky pilots, astronauts have even felt the appeal of home calling to them from up above, in the cold black outback of interstellar space."

—EDWARD ABBEY, *Desert Solitaire*, 1968
(Abbey was born in Home, Pennsylvania)

———

"The developers at the bottom of a pit—that is clear, simple, definitive, and adequately expresses what they deserve. There is no reason to explain further either the opinions about developers or the developers themselves. The word itself, as it comes from the pen, falls like the blade of the guillotine: developers!"

—LOUIS CHEVALIER, *The Assassination of Paris*, 1977 (tr. David P. Jordan)

———

"The old is the best, and the new is of the Devil."

—AMISH SAYING

BIBLIOGRAPHY

HOME TOWN

Ayers, Chuck, and Russ Musarra, eds. *Celebrating Akron's History in Pic-ture Postcards*. Ruth Clinefelter, postcard source. Akron: Sum-mit County Historical Society, 2000.

Bachelard, Gaston. *The Poetics of Space*. Boston: Beacon Press, 1969.

Ellis, William D. *The Cuyahoga*. Rivers of America series. New York: Holt, Rinehart and Winston, 1966.

Francis, David W., and Diane DeMali Francis. *Akron*. Images of Amer-ica series. Charleston, S.C.: Arcadia, 2004.

Izant, Grace Goulder. *This Is Ohio*. Cleveland: World, 1953.

Jonsson, Erik. *Inner Navigation*. New York: Scribner, 2002.

McGovern, Frances. *Written on the Hills: The Making of the Akron Land-scape*. Akron: University of Akron Press, 1996.

Nichols, Kenneth. *Yesterday's Akron*. Seemann's Historic Cities series. Miami: E. A. Seemann, 1975.

Satin, Joseph, ed. *The 1950's: America's "Placid" Decade*. Houghton Mifflin Research series. Boston: Houghton Mifflin, 1960.

ADOPTED TOWN

Barry, Joseph, and John Derevlany, eds. *Yuppies Invade My House at Dinnertime*. Hoboken. Big River, 1987.

Colrick, Patricia Florio. *Hoboken*. Images of America series. Charleston, S.C.: Arcadia, 1999.

Leonard, John, ed. *These United States*. New York: Thunder's Mouth/Nation Books, 2003.

HOME FIRES, BURNING

All quotations from individuals, unless otherwise noted, are from oral history tapes at the Andes Society for History and Culture, Andes, N.Y.

Calhoun, Camilla. "A Town Called Olive." http://www.westchesterlandtrust.org/watershed/olive.htm, 1997.

Duany, Andres, Elizabeth Plater-Zyberk, and Jeff Speck. *Suburban Nation*. New York: North Point, 2000.

Evers, Alf. *The Catskills*. Garden City, N.Y.: Doubleday, 1972.

Frisbie, Richard, ed. *Water for New York City*. Abridged from Edward Hagaman Hall, *The Catskill Aqueduct* [1917]. Saugerties, N.Y.: Hope Farm Press, 1993.

Galusha, Diane. *Liquid Assets*. Fleischmanns, N.Y.: Purple Mountain Press, 1999.

Haring, Harry Albert. *Our Catskill Mountains*. New York: G. P. Putnam's Sons, 1931.

Jacobson, Alice. *Beneath Pepacton Waters*. Andes, N.Y.: Pepacton Press, 1988.

Jacobson, Alice H., and Robert Jacobson. *Echoes Along the Delaware*. Andes, N.Y.: Pepacton Press, 1992.

Kunstler, James Howard. *The Geography of Nowhere*. New York: Simon & Schuster, 1993.

McDonald, Bernadette, and Douglas Jehl, eds. *Whose Water Is It?* Washington, D.C.: National Geographic, 2003.

Merwin, Georgiana. *Once Upon a Time . . . There Was a Cannonsville Valley.* N.p., 1996.

Nash, Roderick, ed. *The American Environment: Readings in the History of Conservation.* Themes and Forces in American History series. Reading, Mass.: Addison-Wesley, 1968.

Sive, Mary Robinson. *Lost Villages.* Delhi, N.Y.: Delaware County Historical Association, 1998.

Steuding, Bob. *The Last of the Handmade Dams.* Fleischmanns, N.Y.: Purple Mountain Press, 1985.

Underneath It All

Lewis Baltz. *Park City.* Albuquerque and New York: Artspace Press and Castelli Graphics, 1980. Photographer Lewis Baltz, with this series, shows everything that I have been trying to get at. The pictures do it with such devastating brevity and precision that I almost wince every time I open the book. (*I don't want to have to go through* that *again.* But I also do, because of their terrible perfection.) They describe the wholesale creation of a ski resort in Utah where there was previously just land—the kind of gorgeous space that once was all of America. They are pictures of a construction site. But what they really capture is our inanity, in the form of what we choose over the landscapes we destroy. Here you see the process, so you can't deny that something better used to be there. When grotesquely cheap architectural abominations sit on top of disturbed soil, amid the debris of their construction, with their poured concrete foundations showing under the tasteless cladding like badly made underwear, you are witness to the full depravity of such actions. Afterward, when the sod has been rolled out and the van is parked outside, it is hard to remember what was here. Lewis Baltz puts it permanently on display, so we can't look away.

ACKNOWLEDGMENTS

THERE ARE MANY for whom I bear deep gratitude. First and fore-most, I would like to thank Google: without you, there would be no book, or a much shorter one. No less am I thankful to Ruth Clinefelter, who read an early version of "Home Town"; Jim Testa of *Jersey Beat*; Chris Tsakis; Nancy Boulin of the Andes Society for History and Culture, Andes, New York; Ron Guichard; the staff of the Cannon Free Library, Delhi, New York; Shelley Wallace of the Paul Cooper Archives at Hartwick College; Steve Pelletier and Dorothy Kubik, who graciously gave permission to reprint their poetry; Mark D. Smith, who is attempting to save parts of Akron that greed would destroy; the Catskill Center for Conservation and Development (and especially Inverna Lockpez), which gave me, in a week's artist's residency in the Platte Clove, the time and space in which to begin. We all have cause to be thankful to former U.S. congressman John Seiberling, who helped preserve a beautiful swath of northeast Ohio in the form of the Cuyahoga Valley National Recreation Area; he also gave me information and general inspiration. And I could not get along without the friendship and sage advice of Jolanta Benal and Sally Eckhoff.

To my mother, thank you for your kindness, support, and love.

My editor, Amy Cherry, has a great ear, a great mind, and a great talent. Thank you for everything and then some. Lucinda Bartley at Norton is ever helpful.

I am grateful to copy editor Timothy Mennel, whose exacting work led to a multitude of improvements.

I have an agent who is the MVP of an All-Star team of one. Betsy Lerner, you are the greatest.

I am at a permanent loss as to how to thank Luc Sante. For there is no end to what he has given me, but it starts with reasons for courage, laughter, true happiness. "Artistic hero" is there on the list. (And to this book he gave a wealth of ideas, not to mention some very fine maps.)

My father was supposed to have read this work and helped correct what I suspect must be its many errors. He did not live to do that. But beyond compiling valuable dossiers to assist my research, lending me books and articles, and answering the many questions with which I phoned him almost daily, he informed the spirit of the entire project. He understood the world that we have been given and helped make and often ruin, and he loved it. And so he gave me the notion, as well as the fact, of home. This book is for him.